D0174965

"I adore this book. Anjuli Paschall has delivered a sacred gift: by sharing her heart on the page, she's shown me my own. In a world tempting us to escape and distract, she invites us to stay and re-member, a practice that ultimately leads us home. This tender, personal book is a timely read for a lonely, doubting generation."

—Emily P. Freeman, *Wall Street Journal* bestselling author
of *The Next Right Thing*

"If you've ever been tempted to run away from life as a grown-up (and honestly, who hasn't?), then this book is for you. Throughout my decades of marriage and motherhood, anytime I've heard the jingle of the ice cream truck in our neighborhood, I've felt the almost unbearable desire to run after it and to just keep on run-ning. Anjuli understands that urge. And she puts into words all the reasons we choose to stay. Nearly two decades into motherhood, I needed all those reminders again today."

—Lisa-Jo Baker, bestselling author
of *Never Unfriended* and *The Middle Matters*,
cohost of the *Out of the Ordinary* podcast

"Endless lists, unrealistic expectations, and needs we can't pos-sibly meet—sometimes life feels like it's just too much. Add in the mess and monotony, the conflict and boredom, and the anger and disappointment, and escape or avoidance feels like our best option some days. But what if, instead of running away, we stayed and sat still in the hardest parts of our lives? What if we got quiet and listened to our hearts long enough to feel what we feel, so we can know what we need?

"In her breathtakingly beautiful debut book, Anjuli Paschall shows us how and why we should stay. Sharing the most vulner-able parts of her soul and her story, my friend Anjuli is the tender warrior-friend we all need, offering unwavering truth and courageous hope that lead us to the truest pieces of who we are and how God really sees us!"

—Renee Swope, bestselling author of *A Confident Heart*, mom of three who has also been known to accidentally take her dog's medication and call the fire department more than once

"Anjuli has written a magnificent and honest book about our deep and also daily pain, and the what-if of sitting with it long enough to experience a love we've unknowingly resisted for far too long. Her words and stories landed like a poem into my heart; they gave voice to my burrowed emotions. *Stay* is a beautifully, vulnerably written invitation to freedom, and I highly recommend it."

—Sarah Mae, author of *The Complicated Heart*

"What does it look like to stay in the moment—no matter how messy, confusing, painful, beautiful, perfect, or imperfect? Anjuli journeys with us into what it looks like to be *real*—and in that place, we find what we are truly looking for: love and acceptance. This is the most important work of our lives, and this is the book that gently and poetically guides us to brave, life-changing places. If you want to change your life, read *Stay*."

—Lisa Leonard, jewelry designer, author, thrift-store lover

"We've all been through circumstances that left us looking for an escape. *Anywhere else but here.* Through her resonant stories, Anjuli vulnerably offers us the sacred invitation to stay. Resist the urge to run and, instead, see the holy significance of this exact moment, this exact place."

—Leeana Tankersley, author of *Always We Begin Again*

"If you struggle with anxiety, disappointment, shame, fear, or false guilt, read Anjuli's story in *Stay* and see your own reflected in a grace-saturated light. Anjuli's relatable writing is fresh and sparkling, and she moves what you know about God's mercy and Jesus's love from your head to your heart."

—Kristen Strong, writer who lives for faith, hope, love, and really good cake; author of *Back Roads to Belonging*

"*Stay* may be the simplest—and hardest—thing to do. We're addicted to being strong and resistant to being needy of God's grace. Bravely and beautifully, Anjuli Paschall invites all of us to follow God into the broken and unfinished places. Her invitation to *stay* is a merciful invitation to *rest*."

—Jen Pollock Michel, author, speaker

"Because of God's love for us, we have the courage to stay—whether that's in ordinary messy motherhood, our emotions, or suffering and pain. Anjuli invites women into this story of the Gospel like a vulnerable friend with a listening ear. May we have the courage to stay put and start small in our corners of the Kingdom of God."

—Ashley Hales, author of *Finding Holy in the Suburbs*, host of the *Finding Holy* podcast, mom to four

"It seems like the opportunity to run away from dealing with our greatest hurts and in turn, our greatest healings, is around every corner. From distractions to purposeful denial, we are all guilty of running away from feelings. This book encourages women to stay and not run, to stop striving for identity in any other place than the hope and healing of Jesus. I am so thrilled for women to read about Anjuli's journey to stay in the uncomfortable feelings we all experience—not for staying's sake, but for meeting the Great Redeemer in it all. This book is a call to all of us to sit with the hurts, the lost dreams, the mundane—and experience being met by God in the deepest parts of our heart."

—Jami Nato, influencer, business owner, speaker, Target shopper

"Anjuli is the most gentle powerhouse. While some might see those two words as a paradox, I see them as the magic that makes up my sweet friend. *Stay* is a reminder that we are never alone and that we are loved more than we could ever imagine—right where we are."

—Manda Carpenter, author of *Space: An Invitation to Create Sustainable Rhythms of Work, Play, and Rest*; foster mom; unashamed Oreo addict

"I wore out a whole pen underlining the gems of wisdom in these pages. For years, Anjuli has ministered to my soul through her steady, calming insights into the heart of our Father. I am overjoyed that more people can have the same experience through this important book."

—Emily Thomas, founder of Mom Struggling Well

STAY

Discovering Grace, Freedom, and Wholeness
Where You Never Imagined Looking

ANJULI PASCHALL

BETHANYHOUSE
a division of Baker Publishing Group
Minneapolis, Minnesota

© 2020 by Anjuli Paschall

Published by Bethany House Publishers
11400 Hampshire Avenue South
Bloomington, Minnesota 55438
www.bethanyhouse.com

Bethany House Publishers is a division of
Baker Publishing Group, Grand Rapids, Michigan

Printed in the United States of America

All rights reserved. No part of this publication may be reproduced, stored in a retrieval system, or transmitted in any form or by any means—for example, electronic, photocopy, recording—without the prior written permission of the publisher. The only exception is brief quotations in printed reviews.

ISBN 978-0-7642-3584-9 (hardcover)
ISBN 978-0-7642-3766-9 (paperback)

Library of Congress Control Number: 2019954214

Unless otherwise indicated, Scripture quotations are from the Easy-to-Read Version. Copyright © 2006 by Bible League International.

Scripture quotations labeled NKJV are from the New King James Version®. Copyright © 1982 by Thomas Nelson. Used by permission. All rights reserved.

Cover art direction by Paul Higdon
Cover photography by Jacob Bell
Cover styling by Sarah Joy Schmidt

Author represented by Alive Literary Agency, www.aliveliterary.com

20 21 22 23 24 25 26   7 6 5 4 3 2 1

In keeping with biblical principles of creation stewardship, Baker Publishing Group advocates the responsible use of our natural resources. As a member of the Green Press Initiative, our company uses recycled paper when possible. The text paper of this book is composed in part of post-consumer waste.

To my children
Manoah, Samuel, Noelle, Hannaly, and Mea Joy
Because I am with you, for you, and I'll
stay beside you till the end.

To my husband, Sam
Because every word written was birthed
from a conversation between us.
I love you.

CONTENTS

Contents

FOREWORD

Though I've never met Anjuli in person (hopefully one day!), I feel like I've known her for years as I've witnessed her life—through images and words online—and now through this book. I was first intrigued by the real and raw way she shares her beautiful and messy journey of motherhood and marriage, finding God in the ordinary, and championing other moms in need. Our worlds intersected even more personally not too long ago when a young mother from our Hope Heals Camp was featured on Anjuli's The Moms We Love Club. This poignant and powerful online community not only brings awareness to the hard stories but invites us to participate in adding tangible goodness to them. Anyone who takes what they've been given and gives it away for the cause of the hurting has my heart. Anjuli's great wisdom online and in this book is in calling us to look outside of our stories to find perspective and purpose as we help those in need, while at the same time challenging us to be brave enough to stay with our whole hearts in our own stories and find them to be good too.

Though disability and all manner of suffering can shatter the life we thought we would have, we see in the life of Jesus the ability to stay in our hard stories and even flourish within them. The book you hold in your hands challenges us to do just that. Anjuli wrestles with so many juxtapositions and invites us to surrender, be vulnerable, and feel the real pain of loss in our stories. While it may not always be easy or enjoyable, the call of the Christian life is always to stay. The problem is that everything in our flesh tells us to run away from pain and suffering.

Neuroscience teaches us that we can train our amygdala—the part of our brain where the fight-or-flight reflex is located—to stay in our pain. We have the ability to train ourselves to stay in the hard stories and not leave, even when our body may be telling us to get out. Isn't that so hopeful!? Just as Jesus stays in our hard and complicated lives, we too can stay and show up for each other.

Equally powerful is the thought that we have the opportunity to stay not only in body but also in soul. The familiar story of the Prodigal Son actually has so much to teach us when we look at the older brother. While the older brother never left his father's side, he absolutely left in spirit. The challenge in our lives is not to be the older brother in our own stories. We must show up not only in body but also with our whole hearts. In *Stay* Anjuli wrestles with how we can show up to the life we have and not the life we thought we would have. She invites us to come out of hiding, to surrender our dreams, to be an outsider, and above all to feel the deep love of a Savior who is with us as we stay.

My prayer for you as you journey through these pages is that you too would feel strengthened and equipped to stay in every arena of your life. May you feel the comfort of a Savior who stays with us and is at work redeeming and restoring everything. May you be inspired and encouraged to show up fully and to wait well. And may you recognize that the mess right in front of you is exactly what God is calling you to live into and love with all your heart until the very end.

Katherine Wolf, author and speaker, Hope Heals

THE WAY HEARTS DIE

An Invitation to Stay

Imagine for a moment you are alone . . . no books, no Netflix, no counters sorely decorated with dishes, no phone.

Imagine there is quiet. The longer you sit, the more you feel. The silence is scary. The argument with your spouse bubbles up to the surface, the sarcastic comment your friend made days ago still hurts, the loneliness you feel in motherhood slices open a shameful hole. Your longings begin to rise. The guilt over not being fully present with your kids rubs you, the loss of a loved one aches, the guilt for not being further along in your spiritual life stings.

The longer you sit, the more your memories take you back to years ago. The anger of your father makes your chest tighten, and the neighborhood boy who teased you incessantly stirs up feelings of embarrassment. All of these complicated memories and feelings make you want to jump up, reply to texts, or reach for a wineglass.

But for a moment, stay.

Imagine the very places you want to fix, avoid, get swallowed in, power through, shout Bible verses at, stuff, or run from are actually the very way to wholeness. Imagine, instead of getting up to investigate what is under the couch or neurotically tidying the mail, you let all those feelings rise. You let them come up to the surface to breathe. You open your heart, talk to Jesus, find love.

Imagine God is inviting you to follow these feelings. Imagine if you could stay with all those unfinished places within your soul and story and let them become your pathway to freedom.

Women's hearts are dying. Right there in the middle pew of our church sanctuaries, our souls are slowly slipping away. It is a vicious pull between doing more and drowning. Life feels like a string of constant disappointments: unpleasant surprises in marriage, friendships dissolving, miscarriages, postpartum depression, months on end with little appreciation and almost no sleep. Our hearts are being wrung out to dry—squeezed and yanked in every direction. Somewhere between signing up for ministry events, checking homework, and making it out of Costco alive, the heart is completely missed, undervalued, and unknown. We walk and move while years go by and we wonder what happened to the person we once knew. A fog rolls in slowly and silently. We live on the surface, somehow just surviving.

But something is wrong. Something is deeply wrong. An uncertainty nestled in our marrow leaves us mute, without words, just a dark, eerie, relentless worry, always there, always present in all we do. We are normal people with normal lives, normal jobs, and normal kids—living as we have been instructed. We've done all the right things: loving, reading, praying, serving, giving, and yet a pervasive dullness drives us to do more, and we've died a million deaths trying to do it all. We know, yes, we know that Jesus loves us in our heads, but we don't experience that in our hearts. We are slowly washing away. I see it in the worn faces of my friends who want to give up on their faith. I see it in the sleep-deprived eyes of women who've walked through tragedy and broken promises and babies who don't stop crying. I've seen it in the persistent demands of perfectionism and pride leading women to put on a performance for more likes on social media. I've lost my true north to politics, pretending, and the pressure to "just be good." We weep, and we don't know why.

In all of our ache, where is the freedom Jesus promised? Where are the streams of living water?

If we've walked with Jesus long enough, we may feel a void inside of us. It feels like a brick wall or an endless dark night, a wilderness or dryness in the spiritual disciplines. It is an uneasy place. One without words. We accepted Jesus into our hearts to escape the void. But it's still there. We know it. It is there inside of us. It makes us feel guilty, ashamed, uncertain, and afraid.

This wall is a barricade between our heads and hearts. The question surfaces: "Why do I know God loves me in my head, but I don't believe it in my heart?" When we hit this spiritual wall, we do one of three things: withdraw, work harder, or walk away. Perhaps not instantly, but slowly. In time, if you don't answer the heart question, you will inevitably pick one of these paths.

When we withdraw, we abandon our very souls because we can't make sense of our inner chaotic cell. Everything inside of us has become too much. There are too many stabbing memories, too much pain, too many confusing God questions, too much undealt-with damage—how could we possibly begin to unpack it all? So we don't. We give up trying. We begin to believe that counseling or Jesus or communion just can't resolve the ache we feel. We keep showing up Sunday mornings, but we slowly disengage our souls. We sit on the sidelines and a deep apathy sets in. We come to accept that everyone else understands this Christianity thing but us. We still believe, but our hearts are passively engaged.

When we work harder, we fight. We battle on, grit our teeth, bear down, and labor on. We read more books, follow more Christian women leaders online, do another spiritual diet, manage our faith with more worship music, and silence all uncertainty. We control and we contain and we constantly lose ourselves in the need to keep up.

When we walk away, we give up on Jesus and the church. There are often deep, unresolved wounds from people or pastors within the church. Our faith becomes a complex and painful story from our past. Jesus just didn't work out.

I know this wall. I have wept here. I've smashed my fist into it until my knuckles bled. I've felt shame here. It's a lonely place. I've begged people to be with me, but it's a place I had to be alone with God. And as I've stayed at the wall with my own temptation to withdraw, work harder, or walk away, I've discovered there is another way.

Perhaps the spiritual wall is actually a work of the Spirit. What if it isn't there because we are doing something wrong, but because God is tending to the soil of our inner world? The process is hard because it means experiencing parts of our stories that make us cringe and collapse. It means painful self-awareness. But the most unlovely parts of us are the very places God is redeeming. God is moving closer. The wall we are pounding upon, tempted to walk away from, or passively disappearing at, is actually a well where Jesus is inviting us to sit with Him, drink life-giving water, and stay.

Yes, stay. Stay where you most resist being.

This staying is a slow and painful sanctification, and it's the place where God is growing us. He is digging a passageway like a tunnel from our heads to our hearts.

We know God loves us like we know there are fifty states. But knowing isn't experiencing. Knowing the names of the states between California and Canada is nothing like driving the Oregon coast during the fall, seeing massive boulders protrude from the sea to the sky or inhaling the heavenly richness of the redwoods. We must understand in our heads *and* in our hearts who God is. We can't just have knowledge of Him, we must experience Him too. If we want to know the love of God in our hearts, we have to be willing to go *into* our hearts. Right theology doesn't make a heart right. The disconnect we experience has little to do with our knowledge of God. More information doesn't maneuver the love of God from our brains to our beating hearts. The connection happens when we stay in our hearts and in the stone-cold silence of prayer. The ache we feel is exactly where God is holding us.

We have to pull up a chair at the table of our souls and invite all of the fractured places within us (the memories, stories, and unpleasant feelings) back together and stay there with Jesus. Only then do we realize that Jesus is the kind host, inviting us to linger, spill the milk, break a dish, be known, and stay, not as guests, but as daughters. He wants to hear our laughter, comfort our ache, ask us questions, and heal our hurts. God, in love, always welcomes us to stay and dine at the table with Him. He is cultivating a home within us.

This is the sacred gift of staying.

Stay is a tender call to enter, to open, and to experience the echoing darkness buried beneath piles of mail and laundry and years of pain. This is a call to follow the fears and frustration to the unknown, frightening places inside. This is a call to uncover. A call to stay. We must stay with the pain. Stay with the anger. Stay with the joy. Stay with the apathy. Stay with the funk and unexplainable feelings. We must stay with the fog. We must feel it heavy on our faces, damp and eerie and dense. We must let the truth of our hearts rise to the surface and accept those wobbly places within us. Christ brings wholeness when the inside of us and the outside of us merge and become one. This is the process of finding words for the places in our past that we never grieved, the feelings that were never fully felt, the sadness that never lessened, the loneliness in marriage we never imagined, or the rejection that rebuffs us over and over and over again. It is remembering who we are. Remembering our story and retelling it again and again and again until our voices don't shake in vulnerability but resound with unyielding strength.

Perhaps your dying heart in that sanctuary is the very pew you are supposed to be occupying. You are exactly where you're meant to be. Not fighting to get ahead and not giving up on ever overcoming, not closing the door on your faith entirely but there, right where you are. Simply opening. Simply accepting. Simply moving inward. Simply staying.

Every scribble of my messy story is how I learned to grow from a young lady to a woman, from single to married, from a wife to a mother. I've given words to the feelings I never could articulate, but only feel. Words about singleness and surrender, marriage and motherhood, aging and dreams being reborn. Words about how I was miserably lost and gloriously found. At each corner of my journey there has been an invitation to enter my feelings and the hard places, the ache and the real me. Invitations to stay at the well with Jesus. This is my story. This is my song. My story is constantly unfolding. But ultimately, my story is about how I learned to become a little girl again, asking a big God if He could stay with someone small like me.

1

CHAPEL AND CHARLIE

An Invitation to Be an Outsider

I went to a private Christian college that sat high on the hills of San Diego overlooking the Pacific Ocean. The college had two types of people: the sheltered, moderately wealthy Christian kids, and the kids who came for the surfing and quick trips to Mexico, who fell asleep in the back rows of chapel. I was the first type, except I wasn't rich (just riding on the benefits of my mom being one of the full-time faculty at the university). I remember the day in August that I moved out of my parents' house and to Point Loma Nazarene University. Moving away from home was exhilarating. The feeling of adventure, independence, and freedom made me giddy, like the first time I earned a paycheck. It felt like standing at the top of a cliff with water below; the thrill of jumping is terrifying, but it is also the same force driving me to leap. I was diving into the world all on my own, though I probably looked like I was falling awkwardly.

College was like living at camp. Instead of recreation, I had class. Instead of free time, I studied. Well, *studying* was a very loose term. If studying meant quick pickup games of ultimate Frisbee or frequent trips to Starbucks, then I was an excellent student. I made friends and pulled all-nighters, and my minivan "Charlie" never had an empty seat when making runs to Adalberto's for a California burrito at midnight or picking up friends at the end of Talbot Street after they skateboarded their way to the bottom. I ran for freshman vice president and, after I convinced a dozen of my guy friends to dress in only towels and dance to "Girls" by the Beastie Boys, I won by a landslide. I tried running (like the actual "move your legs really fast" exercising thing) because all the hip girls went in their cute shorts and high ponytails. I tried it and hated it. Apparently, I'm more of a walking kind of girl. The first week of school a few of us started a tradition—gathering every Monday night at the Greek amphitheater for worship. I poured myself into the hard work of making memories.

By the end of the first few weeks I found my niche, my group, my people. Keri, Pete, Beau, Hans, Allie, Jenni, Chaska, sometimes Jim, and sometimes Andy. They were my go-to friends. Together we could all cram into Charlie, and we did, all the time. Every Friday afternoon we gathered around after classes and laid out all of our weekend options. We all had crushes on each other at some point and irritated each other at others. We were a posse, a pride, a place where we felt connected in all the newness of school.

Midway through my first semester I noticed we all had something in common: the color orange. It was strange but true. Orange happened to be my favorite color, so it was easy for me to pick up on just how much orange people had in their closets. I started something called Orange Wednesday. It was simple. Every Wednesday we wore the color orange, and the trend spread. Within a few weeks the front rows at Wednesday chapels looked like they were draped in orange fabric. Some people wore orange hats and sweatshirts and socks. One of my friends even had orange jeans. It seemed trivial, but really, we were connecting; connecting in even little ways is something big.

To connect, be included, and belong was such a deep desire for me. Despite my desperate attempts to be known, I still felt unknown. I felt like a ghost even when it may have looked like I was the ringleader. People may have seen me as someone on the inside, but I have never felt more like a shadow in all my life. I felt quiet and out of place.

My psychology professor, Helyn Fay, returned my first paper to me with a scribbled note in the margin, "How about you come see me?" So I did. I walked into her office midafternoon. The sun was blindingly strong through the slim, tall windows. She turned to me and welcomed me. She was glad I came. There was something about her countenance that was calming. I felt like I could tell her anything and it wouldn't disrupt her soft disposition. I could tell her the truth. Her compassionate eyes were long arms wrapping me in comfort, but also in protection. I started speaking. I fumbled and nervously tried to express my feelings in actual words. I shared about my insecurities and my inescapable anxiety that made it hard to breathe at times. My knees folded up into my chest as I spoke. It felt so hot in that room. I was afraid. I cried. I laughed. And at the end of our time, she prayed for me.

No one knew how alone I felt. It wasn't just from being at a new school; it was laced in and throughout so many years of my life. I believed that if I could just fit somewhere, maybe I wouldn't feel so messed up inside. And yet there, in the most unexpected place, an office with the sunlight searing me open, I found acceptance. I never wanted to leave. There, with Professor Fay, I found safety talking about the most unsafe things. In that stuffy room, she made a place for my heart to sit down. Surprisingly, my sense of belonging came from admitting how on the outside I really felt.

Belonging isn't about getting on the inside; it's about believing I am loved even while I'm on the outside.

So often I feel the temptation to get on the "inside." I feel a subtle pressure to have the look, speak the language, know the information, and make friends with all the right people to feel like I belong. But over and over again, the invitation comes to stay on the outskirts. Stay with my aging, outdated jeans and never-worthy-enough feelings. Stay with my lack of knowledge, wisdom, wit, and how-to tricks. Stay with my frustration and fear. When I stay on the outside, I start to see the world differently. I see people. The awkward ones, just like me. The ones who don't know how to use a smartphone or who feel nervous (all the time). The ones with complicated stories and dysfunctional families. Belonging begins when I look at a person who has watery eyes and a weary spirit and say, "Yeah, me too."

Belonging is a powerful feeling. It is about being known and accepted and loved in ways we never imagined possible. I'll never forget how found I felt when I was with Professor Fay. I sat in her office week after week for nearly four years. Soon after I graduated, she got sick. I sent her letters and she emailed me when she wasn't in the hospital. I was a guest at a dinner party when I heard she died. I remember running into the bathroom, locking the door, and sobbing with my body laid out on that stranger's floor. I went home and reread our emails. She wrote about how, for her, prayer was like begging for life. I'm not sure I have ever prayed like that before. But I do know that without her, I'd be begging for life in places where life could never be found. She taught me that life is safest when I share it honestly with others, especially the scary stuff. When I stay right where I am, with all that is beautiful and bent out of shape, I find God. I find love waiting for me.

My freshman year I was known for things like my favorite color and Charlie and for being the girl that got boys to dance in towels. Even the simplest points of contact felt like connection, but what I longed for more than anything was to be known in meaningful places. I think we all want that. I found it. I discovered it in my professor with kind eyes who taught me that staying on the outside is actually the loveliest place to be.

The truth is, there was just one type of person at Point Loma: the type who wanted to fit somewhere. We all just wanted to belong.

Belonging isn't about getting on the inside; it's about believing I am loved even while I'm on the outside.

THE GUARD SHACK

An Invitation to Make Mistakes

hen I went away to college, I hoped to leave several things behind me. One thing was a bad relationship. It was a messy and mean relationship, and my only escape was moving. I was also hoping to leave behind the reputation of being a bad driver. I'm not even sure how I earned this title. I had never actually been in a car accident with another car. I may have hit a few objects—like a mailbox and a handful of curbs and an intercom—but never an actual car (or human for that matter).

A few friends in high school absolutely loved to tease me about my driving. I came to church one evening and there were cars lining the parking lot with bumper stickers that said, "I've been hit by a Maneevone (my maiden name), have you?" They thought it would be hilarious to sell these stickers, and I'd see my name posted on cars all around town. I was ready to let the terrible driving reputation be one of those things that stayed in my high school days.

In college I had a flawless driving record until one evening during my sophomore year. Like many schools, ours had a welcome center with a booth and a person standing guard to answer questions and hand out maps or parking passes. On this particular evening my friend was working the "guard shack." I would like to say I had a leg spasm or a bright light distracted me, but it was none of those. Truthfully, I was so delighted to see my friend, I didn't pay any attention to my driving and hit the shack straight-on. *Bump. Thud. Crash.* I was mortified and dreadfully stuck smack-dab into the side of it. Cars were driving by and stopping, filled with friends staring and laughing at my minivan, Charlie, wedged into the side of the guard shack. The worst part was that I actually got a ticket from the campus police, twisting the knife in my pride deeper. I couldn't even bear reading the "cause of incident" section on the ticket: "While waving uncontrollably, she swerved and hit the guard shack."

I had to get towed that night. I called my sister Wanida to come to my rescue, and she did, the way she always does. I had to repeat several times what happened because she didn't understand how I drove into the guard shack and that the van was actually stuck into the side of it. But she came. She didn't ask me to repeat the details of the horrific event again. I slouched down low in the front seat of her Honda. I had had enough of people rolling down their windows, gawking, taking pictures. I was silent all the way to Klassen Hall.

I got out of the car and was making my way toward my dorm when Wanida called out to me. I was halfway down the stairs, and I stopped. She said something like, "It's no big deal; let it go. We all make mistakes—you're human."

Though I can't recall her exact words, I remember exactly how I felt after she said them. It's the way you feel after searching your house for your lost set of keys. You dump out your purse and scramble through the junk drawer and under the couch cushions, and then you find them. You find them on the hook beside the front door, and you smirk to yourself because your keys were in the exact place they were supposed to be, the place you always leave them. I walked down the rest of the stairs and laughed to myself. I laughed at myself for being, well, myself. I laughed because I so easily forget just how human I am and failing is just a reminder of that very thing. A reminder that I make mistakes. Mistakes, as horrible as they feel, are another call to come back to my humanness. A call to come home to my needs and neediness.

I think we all create little idols of our perfected selves. The perfect Anjuli would be fun, outgoing, and spontaneous; I'd be self-sufficient, on time, into yoga, responsible, and have organized drawers. The perfect Anjuli would be generous, loving, passionate, and understand politics. I would be just that, perfect—no flaws, fractures, or faults. I heard it said once that you know you have an idol in your life if someone criticizes you and you quickly crumble or become defensive inside. For instance, if I disappointed some-one, I'd internally collapse because perfect Anjuli meets people's expectations. If I needed to ask a friend to babysit, or to borrow money because I forgot my wallet, or put someone out, I'd feel miserable inside. I'd over-apologize and feel like a burden. I'd come apart because perfect Anjuli has it all together.

Yet God, in love, graciously smashes my perfect-Anjuli idols. One layer after the next, the mistakes I make chip away at my need to be perfect. The walls come down. In the most mysterious way, I think God is in the undercurrent of keeping me close to my brokenness. Drawing me back to that uncomfortable place again and again. God brings me back to the one place where His love can't be earned, only received. His love cannot reach an idol shadow I've created in my imagination. His love can only be absorbed by a real substance, the real me. Me, the girl with a wobbly heart. The one fumbling through life and forgetting her worth. I am incapable of being perfect, but when I encounter my own brokenness, I am brought into companionship with someone who *is* perfection. I am scooped up in the tender mercy of Christ's intentional care of my soul. A love so deep, expansive, and per-sonal that He refuses to let me get caught up in the exhausting effort of proving myself.

I made the mistake of trying to leave behind parts of me in high school. Mistakes are never meant to make us do better next time. Mistakes are meant to be a mirror for me to see who I really am, broken and beloved. I'm learning to be okay with my mistakes. They don't define me or determine my worth, but simply direct me to God.

I'm staying close to my mistakes. I'm talking about them, laughing about them, and learning from them. I'm hugging my cactus and my prickly parts. I am becoming well acquainted with my weaknesses. When my brokenness is met with His loveliness, I can be free, just like that night I crashed into the guard shack, and my sister said whatever it was she said. Mistakes are not my enemy but my guide back to Jesus.

Once there was a little girl learning to ride a bike. She became frustrated that she kept falling and falling. Meanwhile, she watched her little brother jump on his bike and speed away without a single shake. Her dad instructed her in this way: He told her to get on her bike and fall off ten times. She thought falling intentionally was a strange thing to do but followed his instructions and fell off her bike ten times. On the eleventh try she rode all the way to the other side of the street without flinching. Her fear of failure was actually what kept her from riding freely.

I'm becoming familiar with my failings—befriending them, knowing them, hugging them, and being hugged in them—until the ickiness tickles me to laughter. I didn't crash my car ten times so that I could be free, but what I did was this: My senior year I got a job on campus. I sought it out, applied, interviewed, and got it. I worked the weekend 12–5 shift at the guard shack. And when I worked there, I waved at oncoming traffic, and sometimes I even waved uncontrollably.

MY ADDICTION

An Invitation to Neediness

The phone rang. It rang and rang and rang. I let it go to the machine. I stood staring out my front door. I had moved off my college campus to live in a beach cottage with my sisters Leonie and Wanida. We shared a three-bedroom bungalow on Newport Street just blocks from the beach. The night was dark and cold—the wind was exceptionally strong. It whirled right through the screen door. I stood there, wind stinging my face, my heart a wreck, watching and waiting.

The phone kept ringing. I knew he would come. My machine beeped and a frazzled voice spoke. "Adam left. He was driving. He was out of control. He was bleeding and everyone was worried." A similar message came a few minutes earlier. The message told me to call back, but I wouldn't. I'd wait. I waited until the lights of a white Jeep swept past my single-pane windows. It was him.

Adam parked across the street, and I ran. We met in the middle and the world stood still. He collapsed; his face fell into my hands. There was weeping and there was blood and there, in the middle of Newport Street, brokenness bled out all over the pavement. We made our way inside. I wiped his wounds with peroxide and prayer. We didn't say much. I threw away his white shirt spoiled and stained; he fell asleep right there on my living room floor. I turned the lights low and listened to his breathing. He was alive. I fell asleep to the wind hushing and the rhythm of the phone ringing.

Only weeks earlier we had lost time in conversation in the cafeteria. The cafeteria once filled with busyness and bodies, now dwindled down to a table of just Adam and me. We missed class, and our conversation was unsettling. I listened as Adam described how his depression was swallowing him, the sadness unbearable. He started to do poorly in his classes, missing several at a time. He was having roommate problems, and his resident director insisted that he visit the school counselor. He was slipping emotionally. Adam was a cutter. When he was hurting, he cut. When he was sad, he cut. When he was anxious, he cut. His arms were wrecked with jagged, self-inflicted war scars. He cut and cut and cut, but no amount of cutting could heal his pain. He had been warned that if he cut again, he would be asked to leave the school. That night, when he fell in the middle of my street, he had been found cutting again.

Adam was broken and I believed I could fix him. I tried, desperately. Something in me *had* to fix him. I'm a fixer. That is my role. That's what I'm good at. With Adam, healing meant hours upon hours of investing and holding. I had to hold on to him in order to hold on to myself. I've had a lot of Adams in my life. A lot of broken people I found or who found me. And, in time, my own security rested on my ability to rescue. I was a messiah, a girl playing savior to save herself.

I'm not an alcoholic, but I'm an addict. I'm addicted to being the one needed, the strong one. Being the one needed makes me feel significant inside. It's a sturdiness that centers me when I can't control anything else. When my own emotions evade me, confusion scatters me, and conflict threatens me, being needed grounds me. Being there for others feels safe, and right, and Christian.

I grew up in a faith-based home. Billy Graham, Dr. Dobson, and Psalty the Singing Song Book were household names. My parents have spent their lives beautifully ministering to international college students. They tell them about Jesus with hopes that students will return back to their home countries and spread the good news of the Gospel. They've always had an open-door policy. Our home didn't belong to us. It belonged to everyone. People walked right in like they owned the place. I can count the times I heard our doorbell ring as a kid—twelve times. It was a revolving door of people. Students studied in the living room on the weekdays and spent the night on weekends. We shared our fridge with strangers, gave up our beds for the random wanderer, and were last in line to get hot showers. Thousands and thousands of people, from all around the world, have been ushered in and out of my parents' home. There is a sign that still hangs on the wall of their kitchen, proclaiming, "Grand Central Station." Nothing could be truer.

My mom might best be described as a Mother Teresa, Martha Stewart, and Elisabeth Elliot all in one. She is self-giving of her possessions and time, masterfully creative in the kitchen and with her hands, and bold with her faith. When there was a line at a public restroom, she shared the Gospel with the woman in front of and behind her. She was fluent in three languages and earned her PhD when she was 24 years old. Not too shabby for a woman who was already a mom to a toddler and pregnant at the time. All of my life I have witnessed her holding wounded people, putting herself last, being strong, and making room for the hungry and homeless at our table. She gave and loved and poured herself out constantly. I don't think I admire anyone more in the world than my mom. She always made space for others. And since I was her youngest, there was always a spot reserved in all the chaos just for me, right beside her.

"The wound passes through the womb," I heard a therapist once say. The wounds of one generation pass on to the next generation. My mom's unresolved pain became my pain. She had pain she suppressed. She hid it well behind her hospitality and heart to hear others. But the pain slipped out when no one else could see it. It came out when my parents fought. Pain from her own abandonment as a missionary kid being sent away to boarding school before she could read. No one ever told me to push my pain aside and keep a sturdy front. I learned it from my mom. I learned that loving meant stuffing. Loving meant not asking for help and never acknowledging personal needs.

My addiction to being strong likely came from my mom. I adopted her behaviors and skill set (although I've never preached in a public bathroom). It was the wound of my mother and probably her mother and the one before her. Their wounds became mine. My sin addiction to stay strong morphed and took on a unique shape with me. Her motives were probably pure and good, but mine were not. I was motivated to be strong in order to manage my own pain. Sin isn't just doing bad things, it can be using good things (helping others, service, kindness, sex, entertainment, spiritual disciplines, art, adventure, money) to feed the ferocious void inside of us. It is doing everything I can to make life work in my own strength. With the people I tried to save, I was like the bulimic girl counseling the anorexic girl on how important it is to have a good body image. To the same degree that I sought to save others, I secretly longed to be saved. If I could save someone from their misery, fear, or depression, then in my own distress I could be okay too.

The antidote to my addiction is confession. In AA terms, "rigorous honesty." For me, it means admitting my needs. It feels suffocating to confess how needy I am, embarrassing almost. I'm needy for attention, affirmation, and affection. I'm needy to be right, pretty, and praised. I'm needy for love and a hug and time alone. I'm needy for forgiveness, grace, and a pardon for all the things I've done to hurt others. Expressing my needs feels awkward, jagged, painful, and rough — like a teenager learning to drive a stick shift.

I hate feeling my needs; I hate saying them out loud even more. It makes me feel entitled, bossy, annoying, and obnoxious. Yet, Christ keeps leading me back to my need for Him despite my incessant need to run away.

Christ searches my heart, not as a reckless force knocking down my structures of sin, but as a kind shepherd, sitting patient and present. He isn't about ripping up, breaking down, smashing, and managing my behavior, but comes quiet and gently. I am being replanted from a foundation of concrete, tangled cords, and shattered glass to a soil rich with nutrients. A ground that absorbs my neediness as a source for my growth and good.

I wish I could whisper into the heart of that girl holding her fragile friend in the middle of the street, "You don't have to save him to save yourself." It would take years after that night with the phone ringing and the wind blowing and the blood dripping to see just how hurtful my need to save was. I wish I could apologize to all the Adams in my life. I want to tell my mom and my mom's mom that they didn't always have to be strong. Years later, I'm still learning to live in a constant state of confession. I confess that it is horribly uncomfortable for me to be dependent and needy. I feel unworthy, weak, and frail; those things are hard for me to feel. But, God, like my mom, even when there are a million other more important needs in the world to attend to, makes space for me, right beside Him, to be loved.

Christ keeps leading me back to my need for Him despite my incessant need to run away.

THE LAKE

An Invitation to Vulnerability

Something lovely always awaits me at the lake. The endless smooth layer of glasslike water calmly takes me in. Not as a force, but almost as though it whispers to me, "It's safe here." My soul can breathe. My nostrils drink in the smell of a thousand acres of pine trees swaying to a sound only they can hear. I think there is a conversation reserved just for the sky. A language for the sky-souls. The swirling motion of wind, the flap and hush of eagles' arms, and the clouds morphing from inchworms to dragons all exchange kind pleasantries no human can possibly understand. The trees bend back and forth, waving hello to me down below, which I translate into "You came back!"

Generations of feet have tiptoed across the shore. The dock has rocked babies to sleep and bounced boys like rockets into stinging cold water. These waters ripple the reflection of childhood wonder and worn wrinkles. If you listen closely you can still hear all the laughter. It sounds like the recurrent laps of water tickling and turning over the pebbles below, a cheerful chatter, over and over, decade after decade. You can still hear the smack and splash of oars entering and exiting the surface. In these waters, children play in their massive, God-sized swimming pool. These waters have swallowed secrets and broken promises. Vows shattered like monstrous dark clouds overtaking a summer picnic, the earth below the lake becoming a cradle holding buckets of tears. The pines have seen it all. Towering like skinny soldiers, they surround the territory. They've seen each generation rise and fall. All their tree tips like swords pointing everyone upward to God despite the good, horrible, and hard seasons. So much glory. So much grief. Hume Lake holds all my shallow- and deep-end stories, ones from my youth and ones from yesterday.

It is humbling how a single space can hold so much meaning. Hume Lake belongs to millions of people, but I like to think it belongs only to me. If you were a Christian living in California, you likely went to Hume Lake during the hot summers of your youth. Hume Lake Christian Camp has recreation, phenomenal speakers, and the famous milk shakes at the snack shop. Year after year, I recommitted my life to Christ and promised I would keep the fire when I went back down the hill. Year after year, I met a boy and wore his sweatshirt (reeking of puberty) to sleep. If everyone who ever attended jotted their stories on paper and tossed them into the forty-acre body of water, the lake would be overflowing with tales of changed lives, boy heartbreaks, and come-to-Jesus moments.

I worked at Hume Lake during the summer between my sophomore and junior years of college. I grew up and grew deeper in that summer. I met three girlfriends who helped me fill out my very fragile and unknown heart. I went from invisible to visible that summer. Laura, Jenn, and Jessica gave me courage to find my voice. I was suffocating myself with my how-to-be-a-better-Christian laundry list. I suffered from being nice and knowing-the-right-answers kind of Christianity. They taught me what it means to be real, unapologetic, and unashamed.

I sat in a prayer group with Laura. She was having a miserable summer cleaning camp toilets and working lonely hours while desperately homesick. It was my turn to share. My voice hesitated when I asked for prayer. I was constantly saying sorry as if the few words I spoke were a bother to everyone. I was the girl who apologized if you stepped on my foot. But Laura invited me to be real. There in that little prayer circle I felt, for a rare moment, what it was like to be safe.

On our days off, Jenn and I would ride to the other side of the lake, away from the rest of the staff and high school kids and the madness of camp. We snuck away and wore our bikinis (scandalously breaking camp rules). We laid our towels out across huge boulders and soaked in the sun, wearing our bandeau tops and string bottoms. Jenn knew more about the Bible than any other girl I had met, but she wasn't legalistic. She was okay with herself, confident, down to earth. And as we laid out every Tuesday afternoon in the heat of the summer, we talked about God, college, and dreams while letting the sun darken our bare shoulders.

Jessica and I were inseparable. We shared a bunk and our lives. We hung our feet off the dock after the sun set and the moon rose. We prayed and sang and stargazed. I'll never forget the night when I found my sweet friend sobbing in the corner of the canteen. She was rocking, knees close to her chest. A boy she loved didn't love her back. He ended things, and it ended her. I sat down right beside her on the coffee-stained, sticky floor, and we wept to the sound of coffee blending and high school kids doing open mic.

These friends stirred me to speak honestly, to break the rules, and to sob even if people were watching. They taught me how to be honest. It's not that I was lying; I just didn't know what it meant to be vulnerable. Oftentimes I think we confuse vulnerability with something we do. But vulnerability isn't something we choose to do; it is who we are. I'm not talking about gender, race, sexuality, ethnicity, family name, or title. I'm talking about who we really are as beloved dust, birthed from a word, brought to life from a breath, imperfect children of God. It's who we are way deep down at the bottom of ourselves. We are vulnerable, humanity's great equalizer.

We cover and clothe our vulnerability with anything we think will protect us. We keep a cautious distance from anything that threatens danger. Paradoxically, the opposite is true. I am only safe when I stay in my vulnerability *with* God.

I can be who I am: stripped down, weak, exhausted, under-whelming, insignificant, hopeless, hurting, and afraid because in the fragility of my inner world, I am gathered up by God. I am beloved, held, secure, safe. I become gloriously worthy and graciously met in the middle of my vulnerability. If there is no love, my vulnerable state is helpless. I need love like I need air. Without vulnerability, I am unable to experience God's love. Vulnerability is the pathway to intimacy. It's the only way. It is terrifying, but true.

The Maker of all mankind, sea, sky, earth, and outer space is calling me out into the water. There is a revolving invitation to "Come." *Come* isn't just an action that requires more work or one more thing for me to do. *Come* is also an invitation to let what has been pushed under water and buried inside rise up to the surface. When I let what has been hiding come up, it is like I step onto the shore; my soul, like this lake, is exposed. I let my secrets come into the safety of light. I let my disordered desires be seen. My overeating, overdrinking, overspending—I let them all rise up. My secret happiness at others' failures, my indulgence in gossip, my quest for influence—I let it all be known. I risk that the water, like a whale, will rise and swallow me in one gulp like it did Jonah. But I watch how the water rests effortlessly in the cupped hands of God's created dirt. God invites me to be as vulnerable as this lake, held in the soil of His sovereignty. When fear presses down over me, I uncurl my chest and stretch out my spine. I pry back my body and open all of me to Him. I resist my tendency to defend, attack, protect, and panic. My soul's discipline in surrender is to relinquish life on my terms.

I let go of my need to control my life and even my death. A peace rushes over me, knowing that no matter what has happened or happens—cancer, tragedy, rejection, loss, grief, accident, or worst-case scenario—I am safest, right here, vulnerably trusting Jesus. The words almost spill out of me: "Thy will be done." I am always met in love. God, welcoming me, like the trees, into a safety as strong and kind as the mountains bowing down like a gentleman greeting the water's edge with a kiss.

5

NAKED MANGO EATING

An Invitation to Your Loneliness

Mangoes stain. When summer whisked its way through my childhood home encircled by an orange grove and my dad brought home a Costco-sized box of the smoothest, freckled-skinned mangoes, my mom would shoo my sisters and me outside. Instinctively, we stripped down to our undies. With our bare brown skin exposed to the sun, we sat on our concrete steps, our dirty feet tapping in giddy repetition. My mom placed freshly cut halves of sweet, dripping mangoes into our eager little palms. We sucked ripe mangoes until the juices stained our cheeks and the strings went like floss through our teeth, sending shots of nectar into our gums. There was something glorious about devouring summertime fruit in our unmentionables and letting heat dry sugar love to our skin. Our sisterhood grew on the scent of orange blossoms, music, and the joy of naked mango eating.

My three older sisters are all I have ever wanted to be. They are each unique, beautiful, and vibrant with personality. My oldest sister, Leonie, is smart. It might be more appropriate to say brilliant. The kind of girl who never studied but showed up on test day to destroy the curve. Malina is as sparkly as Fourth of July fireworks. She is bursting with the most infectious love for life. Wanida, two years older than I am, has boundless creativity. When she sings, her voice opens your soul into a canyon of awe and anticipation. One would think that being the fourth girl in a family like ours would create a dark shadow over me, a heavy weight to bear. But I never experienced my sisters that way. They were my refuge, my shield of protection, my shade.

I wanted to be my sisters. I wanted to laugh, love, and look like them. As long as I could become like them — beautiful, spontaneous, whimsical, generous, and endearing — I would be okay. And I was okay, or at least I thought I was okay. My sisters were my light, and I hovered around them like a firefly circles a burning candle, desperate for life.

I attached myself to my sisters. I used their affirmation, attention, and adoration to fill my lonely places. I used them to fill my vacant soul spaces. Sometimes I imagine my heart is like a massive rubber band. The stretchiness of the band-like heart muscles will wrap around anything (I mean anything) — words, people, events, acts of kindness, spiritual disciplines, dreams, or likes on a Pinterest picture — that will mirror back to me meaning, significance, importance, beauty. My rubber-band heart needs an object to worship me back and to tell me who I am or that I'm okay. My rubber-band heart clings to those objects like a lifeline, consuming them until it snaps and stings. Then I find another object to wrap my heart around. My soul is desperate for company so I don't have to experience the agony of being alone. For as long as I can remember, my rubber-band heart has wrapped around my sisters, keeping them in arms' reach, close by, strapping down and stitching shut my anxiety and fears.

After college, I worked in the inner city of Bangkok with a few friends. Near the slums and city streets, we played with the poorest of the poor children who were without shoes or shelter or front teeth. We taught English in the evenings and built houses on the weekends. On the evening of the full moon in the twelfth month of every year, the Thai celebrate a holiday called Loi Krathong. Translated into English it means "floating decoration." Shop vendors spend days creating and designing floating baskets that they sell on every street corner—baskets weaved from the trunks of banana trees and spider lily plants. Banana leaves are braided around the baskets, poked with incense, ignited with candles, and decorated with coins. The most delicate flowers crown the basket, creating an offering of beauty to be sent down the river. Historically, the light gift represented repentance for wrongs that had been done and celebrated new beginnings. Thais believed water gods would give them a do-over. But now it is simply a fun festival of light that brings young and old together.

Loaded into the back of pickup trucks with children on our laps and the smog of city traffic in our faces, we raced to the nearest river, with our light offerings in hand. We could see people for miles leaping off of scooters and tuk-tuks. Kids in ragged clothes and adults in flip-flops all running down dirt roads to the river. Past houses with slanted tin roofs and stray dogs, dodging mud puddles and trash piles, we ran. I slid down the side of the riverbank, looking out into water rippling with the loveliest baskets, a parade of lights, the musk of incense burning my senses and the glow of candles begging their beauty in exchange for a pardon. With my toes touching the edge of the water, I pushed my banana leaves and budding flowers into the current. I watched my basket disappear, a single flame joining a wildfire.

In that moment, with children chasing after their offerings, laughter erupting all along the darkness of the riverbank's twists and turns, and a glorious tapestry glowing with the fragrance of hope, all I could sense was just how miserably alone I felt. Even in a crowd of people my presence felt so small. When I watched that candle drift downriver and I stood hiding in the shadows of mango trees, I felt what I so often felt but pushed away for so long: the relentless feeling of loneliness.

That night on the side of the river I felt what I had been dreading my entire life: The noise of that lonely place inside of me was getting louder. That desperate lull and hum that I experienced only when I was alone was now escaping into my real, everyday, and busy life. I couldn't shut it down or selectively put away the ache. I couldn't close the gaps between my real internal world and my outer world any longer. I couldn't manage my loneliness. I was starting to experience the one thing I hated experiencing the most:

me. It was painful self-awareness. The only thing I didn't know how to deal with or explain or understand was me. I hid behind my sisters for so long. When I didn't know how to deal with me, I attached to them to feel safe.

But that happens sometimes, doesn't it? We get lost in other people, hoping they will save us, wrapping our rubber-band hearts around anyone and anything we can. We give our light away to friends and family members. We do things like idolize people and make heroes and hope we can piggyback on their strength to get us through. We hang our identities on a rope, hand off the other end to someone we believe has the power to save us, then jump, dangling over a cliff, begging our superhero, spouse, sister to save us — to never let go, to stand there holding our hearts over a ledge.

That's what happens when we get enmeshed, when our identities get lost in someone else's, when we don't know where we end and where they begin. For a brief moment, it feels so wonderful to get lost, to sense that powerful connection and companionship and sacredness. But the danger broods silently, just below the surface. Like being beyond the breakers at sea, there is a quiet but unsettling feeling; even in the vast beauty we sense a murmur, "Something isn't right." Because something in our souls was made for intimacy with identity, not absent from it.

So often, even in my relationship with Jesus, I am hiding my true identity from Him. How different is my prayer life than that of my Thai ancestors? How much of my prayer life is a ritual, saying the right words and doing all the right things on the right day?

Sending out something beautiful into the world just hoping to be loved and let off the hook in return. I come before God and others all put together. I take time curating and creating an offering that is suitable. I send it away, hoping that I've done enough to earn favor in return. If my offering is received, then I am free. I wrap my hopes into the threads of a pretty prayer and like that basket I float it down a river, desperate for God to receive me. When I feel worry ripping through the concrete corridors I've created, I quickly pray it away, thinking that my magical prayers will lock those scary feelings back into their cage. When I don't want to deal with the reality of me—my anger, fear, or out-of-control feelings—I recite a memory verse on repeat, thinking it will fix me. I turn the worship music on a little louder in the car, drowning out my real feelings of jealousy or lust or despondency.

Because, really, all the magical prayers and ritualistic disciplines stem from my desire not to deal with the real me. I want a Hail Mary prayer to make all the thorns in my internal landscape as pretty as the roses I buy at the farmers' market. I just want God to make me better, stronger, sweeter. I push the ugly down and present a floating prayer to the skies.

My grandparents worked with the Dalai Lama in the mid '60s. They were missionaries working near the border between Tibet and India. When Tibetans were horrifically pushed into India, my grandparents embraced many of the displaced refugees, including the Dalai Lama, his family, and his secret service. Since then, my grandparents have affectionately been loved by the royal family and his close friends.

I had the opportunity to sit down with the Dalai Lama in a private meeting. A few family members and myself waited hours and passed through long lines of security before we were ushered into his room on a secret floor of a San Francisco hotel. He was kind and delighted to see my grandma again. They put their glasses on and leaned over aged photos like they were looking into a time tunnel taking them back to their younger selves. They shared stories of when the Dalai Lama and his family were in exile from Tibet and taking refuge in India.

The Dalai Lama took time to walk around the room and greet each of us, one hand extended to ours and another holding a card with a Tibetan wish. As he came to me, he read the blessing aloud, "*rlung lang po*," and out of nowhere, he burst out laughing. His eyebrows nudged for his translator to explain what was so funny. The blessing card given to me meant, "You will never be angry again." The Dalai Lama pinched my chin in familial tenderness. He knew, I knew, and the entire room knew that no amount of wishful thinking or a blessing on a piece of card stock could take anger away. And there in that locked-down penthouse high above San Francisco Bay, the Dalai Lama and my closest family let out a giant belly laugh that, despite our religious differences, we all knew that anger doesn't flippantly disappear.

No amount of wishful thinking or magical prayers work because those aren't relational, and God is only about relationship. It isn't a ritual that will take away the painful truth of who we are; it is a relationship. It's not the pregame ritual; it is the coach coming to bat beside you, talking you through the errors, helping you see how your stance is off balance and your elbow needs adjustment. God is always interested in revealing truth. His truth encounters our truth; it is only there that we can be loved. God isn't particularly looking to take our loneliness away, but to fill it with himself.

God allows the heart rubber bands we've wrapped around people and objects to snap. When that happens our hearts feel the whiplash, and it hurts like crazy inside. When a relationship breaks, when escrow falls through, when the business goes bankrupt, when approval is never earned, when our adult children don't return calls or come over, it destroys something deep inside of us. When the very thing we think will complete us doesn't come to completion, a magnificent task sits before us. If we aren't careful we will lash back because the pain hurts so bad. Our temptation is to get revenge at God or others. We shut our hearts off to God when life doesn't go the way we think it should. In our relationships we smirk when they gain weight or lose a job or a marriage hits a wall. We are tempted to rejoice in their sufferings. But if we are careful, very, very careful, we will wait. We have to let the ache be exposed.

We have to stay with the pain.

We have to let all the nerve endings rise to the surface and let the stinging make us weak. This is where we meet God. Right in the middle of our everyday ache and deepest wreckage. The pain that we are so tempted to fill in our own power has to lay trembling and open before Jesus. When we stay, He comes. We have to be real with God in order to find real help from God.

My loneliness needed to be explored, felt, understood, and filled. The Spirit, alone, offers deep companionship. The rubber bands I wrapped around my sisters had to be cut. One by one, He cut the stranglehold I had on them. My co-dependency snapped. The process was painful because when I didn't grab on to them, I had to feel just how deeply alone I was. The rubber bands I wrapped around my sisters, God wanted wrapped around himself. I couldn't love my sisters freely until I set them free. He wanted to fill the voids and vacancies within my soul. He wanted to enter my emptiness. God is only interested in filling our darkness and bringing new life.

God wraps the wildest, unbreakable, expandable heart rubber band around us. One that never severs no matter how far it is stretched. It entered the depths to reach us. Jesus, bending low, entering earth, wrapped us in His love and brought us back to God. He rescued us from our loneliness and filled us with His love and compassion. Like a boomerang, His rubber band brings us back to the Father's heart. We press our ear to His chest and find the greatest friendship known to mankind. God longs to free us from the people and things we use to fill us apart from Him. When we rest in His presence, we are finally full. When our identities, our heart rubber bands, wrap around His identity and His around ours, neither best friends nor brothers, religious leaders nor mango-stained sisters can diminish our fire. Our loneliness is filled with the warm companionship of God our Father.

When we stay,
He comes. We
have to be real
with God in order
to find real help
from God.

FOX ISLAND

An Invitation to Feel Pain

D ays after my twenty-fourth birthday, I boarded a plane from San Diego to Seattle. I was getting on a direct flight, then driving down to a small city called Gig Harbor to meet a man who could help me with, well, me. It was a retreat designed to deal with the dark places, the hidden, the secret, the lonely places. It would be three weeks of isolation.

Three weeks without internet, phones, or texting. Three weeks of fasting from coffee, exercising, and entertaining. Three weeks, alone, in a cabin. Nothing but me, my pain, my past, and my Bible. With the help of a therapist, I would plunge into my memories of pain in search for feeling. The retreat was designed to deal emotionally with childhood pain that had been thought through, but not actually felt. Digging, digging, digging graveside, ferociously fighting against earth, and mud, and decay to get to the dead bones. Screaming, attacking, beating, and battling my demons until I didn't just know my pain, but felt it. It meant putting my parents in an imaginary chair and having arguments I never had with them before. It meant yelling until I lost my voice or breaking bottles or doing whatever it took for me to actually feel.

We all have a dam inside of us that trickles life-giving water, running through the cracks. The three-week retreat was meant to set off a bomb inside the interior walls I had built, sending the rocks of my dam bursting apart, making a way for streams of living water to flow effortlessly and free.

To say I was nervous about the bomb exploding inside of my chest was a slight understatement. I was terrified.

I was afraid of being alone, of losing my faith, of finding feelings I didn't know how to deal with. I was afraid of God, of my anger, of my past, but more than anything, I was afraid that nothing at all would happen, that I would spend three weeks in isolation, violently re-entering pain that I spent my entire life running away from and come out more broken than I was going in and with fewer answers.

There is something unsettling about life with no answers. Something hopeless, defeating, and devastating. When the layers have been peeled back and you sit in the absolute question of life and God and death, there is a nerve-racking reality that each of us is totally alone. It's like the cold feeling I get in my chest when I start to imagine how massively boundless space is and how deep the depth of the sea is. This place called Earth is like a teeny tiny speck of nothing. We are but dust. I was alone from birth and alone before stepping foot into that cabin.

I had been questioning my faith and finding that the more I entered my own disillusionment, the more pain I unpacked, leaving me raw and lost. God seemed absent; it was as if my prayers hit the ceiling then fell right back down again. Reading the Bible felt like trying to swallow cotton: dry and miserable and impossible. I kept waiting for God to do something in my life—kept waiting for Him to show up—but I felt empty no matter how much I worshiped or prayed or served. Nothing seemed to smooth out the ruggedness I felt inside. Nothing seemed to snap me out of my funk or dysfunction.

I remember my first night in the little cabin on Fox Island, just above the Wollochet Bay, looking on into what felt like forever. I remember over the water there was a haze, gray with a hint of glowing, from the light burning through the remaining clouds. I remember thinking that if my biggest fear came true after three weeks here, then I'd have to walk away. Walk away from Christianity, from my beliefs, and from life as I knew it. I couldn't keep living.

I met with Bryan, a therapist, once a day for an hour and a half before going back into isolation. Bryan was kind and quiet and good. He listened and waited and prayed. And like a doctor with a patient in surgery, he handled my pain with precision and delicacy, dealing with my wounds as a matter of life and death. During my first week it felt like torture. I was at war with myself. I was fighting constantly with my demons, stabbing at shadows, and wrestling with my weaknesses like someone switched the garbage disposal of my soul to on.

I spent hours journaling, hours weeping, hours letting my rage ramp up. It felt like I had to mentally brace myself before entering this madness, like bracing yourself before the roller coaster takes off: You check your seat belt one more time, look around at your friends, and mentally prepare yourself for the crazy ride, not knowing what awaits. Then when the ride was over, I'd exhale, get off the ride, and check out—doing things like taking long baths and scrubbing floors and plucking my eyebrows.

This routine of fighting and checking out went on for days, but truthfully there was never reprieve; everything was work. Work was surfacing as a theme in my life. I worked at being a good daughter. I worked at being a good friend and a good person. I worked at being a good Christian.

All of my life was work; this work was killing me. I was so tired of working, so tired of me. Bryan said things in our sessions like "True religion is about eating when you are hungry and sleeping when you are tired." He told me a story about a fish swimming frantically for the magic ingredient that sustains life. One day the fish, filled with anxiety and fear, found a wise old fish that told him the life-giving substance was called "water." All the fish ever had to do was just swim. I reread Matthew 11:30, where Jesus said, "My yoke is easy and My burden is light" (NKJV). These phrases and verses touched my torment, but it was as if I were trying to thread a needle, and the stories kept missing the eye of my pain. So, I kept trying to work through the pain, kept fighting with the imagined image of my father in the rust-orange rocking chair, kept searching for the substance called water, kept carrying the rocks on my back until the afternoon of day fourteen.

It was noon and the August heat penetrated through the single-pane windows. It had been another morning spent spinning my own web of self-inflicted torture. As the sun hit its peak something changed. For a moment I could stop, step back, and see something that startled me. In the middle of my rage, I saw my self-hate. Within those cabin walls, I saw how religiously I beat myself up. I was the ascetic whipping myself into being better. When I saw this it really surprised me — the way a clunk and rattle inside your engine makes you stop, lean in closer, and listen.

I remember lying on the ground, eyes closed, imagining me at four different seasons of my life: a little girl, a teenager, a young adult, and my current twenty-four-year-old self. With my eyes closed, this is what I saw: a girl in all these different ages floating in a wooden canoe down a river like the Lady of Shalott, dying. I watched myself being washed away to the sea. I wanted to die. I, in that moment, hated who I was, who I had always been, hated me in every season of my life.

Self-hatred had been what kept me alive; it was driving me. Dying in that wooden vessel actually brought me peace. I didn't have to work anymore. I could give up. I could end everything. And that afternoon in August, I peered into the depths of my self-hatred. I saw it, accepted it. I wondered what it was about me that I hated so much and why dying felt like freedom.

The answer wasn't complex or profound. It was simple. It was as simple as the chorus of "Jesus Loves Me." It was this: I was a sinner. I was a sinner and I couldn't save myself and I hated everything in me that tried and failed.

I gathered myself off the floor, slipped on my shoes, and went for a walk. I was a sinner. I let this sink in as I walked through the streets of the forgotten island. Over a hill sat a field with horses, strong and gracefully grazing through the grass. I sat on the edge of a fence and found that for the first time in two weeks—perhaps in my entire life—I was at peace. True, deep, abundant peace. I was a sinner unable to save myself.

The self-hatred that powered me to work harder was laid to rest. And as I watched the horses, I saw two figures walking toward me. I wasn't sure what to do. I had been in isolation for two weeks and hadn't talked to or seen another soul except for Bryan. But I stayed composed on the rickety wooden fence and waited till they stood right beside me. An older woman and her daughter looked at me with confusion, but also awe. The mother asked me my name and I replied. I fumbled to get down off of her fence. Then she said something I'll never forget. She asked me, "Are you an angel?" She said she drove by me and when she saw me sitting on the fence, she thought I was an angel and had to come talk to me. How could I ever explain to this stranger that in the very moment she thought she saw an angel she actually saw a girl accepting her sin for the first time? And right then by the fence with this stranger, all of the pieces came together like fingers folding to pray: my life fitting into place. I was, am, a sinner and God was, is, my Savior. When I know who I am, all anxiety and hatred and fear fall deafeningly silent. I am seen and coated in His glory, a glow that beams like the angels.

I think we live our lives like a movie. There is a comedy in all of us and a romantic story line that trumps any Hollywood chick flick. There is a horror film that makes us shudder, and when the terrible scenes surface in our memory we shut them down, push pause, or slam off the DVD in our minds. We live our lives in the beautiful and sometimes tragic reality that the beginning of our story determines the end of it. I can't just keep the parts I like, those moments when I made a room full of people laugh, when I received my diploma or danced down the streets of Paris. I can't edit out the scenes I hate like the time I peed in front of my entire first grade class during show-and-tell or when I sat in a parking lot, alone, weeping in sync with the waves hitting the shore. I spent most of my life playing the scenes I loved on repeat and stuffing the scenes I hated into a dark dungeon. All the bad things that have happened to me I stamped with a label, "already dealt with that. No need to fix anything here. What's done is done."

But we are people, not machines. We operate on a level far beyond any function button on a remote control. We breathe and live and our hearts attach desperately to experiences in our lives. When we shut out our past, we shut down our ability to be healed, to be whole, or to understand God's love for us in the depths of our hearts. We live half alive.

The feeling of God's absence in my life was not because of His actual absence. He was present, deeply and more intimately than I ever imagined. He allowed my attempts—my work—at spiritual disciplines to become laborious and dry. "Doing" my faith was futile. God didn't remove the feeling of His presence because He was punishing me. No, He was inviting me into maturity, into greater relationship and growth.

When I didn't feel Him, I felt me. I felt the pain of me, the truth of my motivations and my corrupted ways of meeting my own needs and trying to manipulate others and God. In all the feelings of absence, He actually was allowing me to see myself, to see the deep me, the real me, the me He really loved. The me that only did the disciplines to be the good girl and get off the hook for my bad. He was purging me of falseness and secret sins, and pushing away my pain. He wasn't letting me hide behind the song and dance of all my Christian deeds. He wasn't satisfied with my sacrifices; He sees past all of that and pursues the heart. The way-down-there, silent, messy heart that is so carefully hidden from others and even me.

His love won't stop till the hidden heart is known and loved. He is rigorous to reveal our hearts. He fights for it. He died to get it. He allows pain and joyless disciplines and brokenness and heartache and loneliness to excavate a path for His love to get all the way to the black bottom of us. He is the master archaeologist, digging, tearing, opening, and discovering until what was lost is found. Because unless the heart is known, it can never be loved. It can never be free.

This is the power of staying.

After three weeks alone, I learned that I wanted to be fully alive, deeply and passionately alive. I didn't want to shut down the parts of me I hated anymore; I wanted those places to be what made my heart thick and lush and gritty with real life. I learned that pain is a gift. It is a glorious, ugly, and dangerous gift. A gift that if not handled with gentleness and grace can cause more damage. Pain requires a companion, a comforter, a counselor. Pain is the doorway to hope, to redemption, and our redeemer.

Pain has been infused into our bones since the beginning. It was there in the fall that the hearts of all mankind became twisted. Our hearts became bent, and with every scene of our lives the twist intensified. We chip away at the massive wounds—branches, gnarled this way and that—with a toothpick, thinking that our tools and tactics can undo the damage. Tools like fashion and humor and the number on the scale or the completed checklist or being perfect. We think these tools have power to bring peace. But the twisting stitches our chests tighter and tighter until our breath becomes labored and our bodies limp. So we change our tools and we become more dependent on our toolbox. We depend on alcohol or medication or our sexuality or marriage to keep the thorns from choking us to death. But we've already been dying since day one.

There is a secret to the untwisting of all those branches binding us. It is the secret I found on Fox Island in that cabin overlooking the blue Wollochet Bay. The secret found me. The secret came to that girl hitting the floor, the girl hating herself, the girl damning all of her past to the pits of hell. The secret came to me on a long wooden fence as the wind blew my hair and the golden hour of light laid to rest upon the field of grass below my dangling feet. The secret was that Jesus carried the twisted branch upon His shoulders, He walked down a long, dusty path to a hill. And that branch bore the weight of His body. The twistedness of an entire world of brokenness bled down the branch. And when His body breathed its last breath, all of humanity breathed its first.

And that's what I did my last night on the deck of that cabin, alone, in that rocking chair. I breathed. I breathed for what felt like the first time. I breathed like eternity was inside my chest. I breathed so deeply that I could feel and hear my heart beating. I was whole. I let that girl in the boat sail out to sea. I let her die; she, with her self-hatred and do-good Christianity, died that day. And perhaps that's what Jesus meant when He said you have to die in order to truly live. I looked inside of me and all the knots and twists and torment that once crippled me now formed the very path that caused me to see who I was and who was in me. I breathed. Over and over like oxygen was filling my soul, like drinking living water, like the woman at the well asking for more. I was free.

His love won't stop till the hidden heart is known and loved. Unless the heart is known, it can never be loved. It can never be free.

7

THE COFFEE SHOP

An Invitation to Listen

We sat in the coveted corner seat, the two-seater table right beside the window. It was tucked away, almost out of sight, sheltering our conversation from the constant swing of the coffee shop door. Zanzibar Coffee Shop is in Pacific Beach, one of the many San Diego coastal cities. This one is where the beach bum and the hipster high-five. Salt water meets skinny jeans. College kids own the streets, shopping at the whole-foods corner stores, meeting up for sushi, sharing their most recent homemade beer concoction. The place pops with color. Alleyways are lined with political murals and the underbellies of bridges grumble with a thousand opinions scribbled with spray paint, artistry, and anger. Music ushers along the dozens of feet shuffling the sidewalks. As all the world rushed and pushed and played past the window, our fingers hugged our coffee mugs in a tight, awkward tension.

Drew and I had dated for three years. We met in college and our chemistry was instant. We managed to stay committed even after graduation while I was traveling abroad and while he was jobless and poor. We went through a premarital course and talked about marriage, kids, and careers. Throughout our entire relationship there was always one glitch. I wanted to go into missions, abroad or locally, and Drew wanted to make movies. He used a camera, light, humor, and thoughtful dialogue to make beautiful films. He didn't want to move overseas; I didn't want to move to Hollywood. I was going to seminary, and he was applying to film schools. There was a constant push and pull between us as we tried to figure out how to make our two different paths one. I couldn't change his dreams; he couldn't change mine. After three years of dating, we met in a dark parking lot, eyes wet and stinging as we looked out over the blurry San Diego skyline. I ended things. So much of me died that night. After all the memories and the pictures lining my bedroom wall, I was letting go—sending away—what made so much of me. That night in the parking lot was nine months prior to this evening gripping our coffee mugs at the coffee shop.

There was friction between us. An uncomfortable feeling of being with someone I had known so intimately, but who now felt like a stranger. As loud college kids filtered in and out of the Zanzibar Coffee Shop, we sat in silence with racing hearts. We were dabbling with the idea of getting back together, of giving "us" another go.

It was a conversation we had on the calendar, one we knew would be significant, and one that we were possibly avoiding because the seemingly inevitable, permanent end to our relationship was more obvious than ever. We sat in that overcrowded coffee shop and took turns sharing. I went first: I shared my dreams. I laid out a passion that was inside of me like the air I breathed. I was following a road of education, coming alongside people in their brokenness. I went on and on about starting a retreat center and a holistic approach to wholeness—physically, spiritually, and mentally. I shared, not trying to change him or convince him, but because it flowed out of me effortlessly. He listened and affirmed me. He let out a deep sigh of acceptance, as though, with a breath, he was letting us go.

He shared about grad schools and how he was writing a screenplay and how much he hated LA but that he knew it was where he was headed. I listened—for the first time. I listened for him and not for me. I listened to his heart and hopes and fears of entering a career that has a lot of casualties and some dismal rates of success. I could hear him, not for what I was going to gain or lose, but because I was done controlling and trying to jam our lives together.

When Drew was done sharing, the strangest thing happened. In that crowded coffee shop, we didn't hear a single sound except the grind of coffee blending. Our eyes scanned the coffee shop, curious with confusion. How on a busy Friday night was this place silent? The coffee shop was filled with people, yet there were no words spoken. Instead, adults sat and stood, using their hands to speak. That night, the coffee shop was a gathering place for those who were deaf. All around us, people used hand gestures instead of words. Drew pulled out a little notebook and jotted down this moment, something he did when he wanted to remember an experience for a future storyline in a film.

I go through most of life not listening to others, or what my mom calls "selective listening." I hear what I want to hear. I listen with hooks and "if-then's." I ask people, "How are you?" and feel interrupted when they actually answer. So often I go out into public to prove something to someone. I am quick to use wit or deflecting tactics or my children to maneuver my way through a crowd. I calculate conversations like a game of chess. I presume and assume another's thoughts and jump at the chance to offer advice. I interrupt and intrude with my idea of what they should do. I dole out judgments and passive forms of encouragement. When their words dip into unsafe realms, I try to buoy them up and out of the unknown places within their hearts. I nervously scramble to fix them or keep them from sinking into their own darkness. I have a hard time being with others because their pain triggers my pain.

Listening, really listening, is like learning another language. Listening is a risk. It can be a scary space. It requires releasing control. It requires really staying with a person as they are, not as you think they should be or want them to be. It means letting go of things going my way. No amount of my good behavior, well-crafted sentences, or perfectly managed words can manipulate another person's experience. I've spent most of my life believing I had the power to make people happy and protect how people perceive me. The older I get, the more I realize I have no such superpower. I don't have control over how people feel or the choices they make. I don't know what they ought to do, steps they need to take, or a solution to their struggles. I don't.

It's hard to be with people, really with them. We tend to have hooks and layers of selfish ambition laced into every sentence. We are afraid of being rejected, misunderstood, or manipulated. It's hard to hear when fear, anxiety, and my neurotic need to control are so loud. But what I can offer is me, all of me. Me, with my messy motivations. I can offer my presence, my attention, my compassion. I can be curious and ask simple questions. I won't be perfect, but I'll be enough. I can acknowledge their pain and stay with them in it without passively trying to fix them. Listening allows me to enter another person's story with grace and not as a know-it-all. People deserve grace. It's an honor to be invited to hear tender parts of their stories. I don't know how long I have with another person. It could be five minutes or fifty years. But I do know I want to attend well to others.

Listening requires a third ear, the heart. My two ears listen to another and my heart listens to God. As I listen to others, I'm also listening to God for discernment. I ask for His help to ease my anxiety and help me see this person the way He sees them. Perhaps the greatest gift I can ever give anyone is to see and listen to them the way God does. I can stay with them as God stays.

That night at Zanzibar Coffee Shop, I was learning how to stay with my dear friend unattached from needing to gain or get something. I spent so many years being deaf. At the coffee shop we listened. We let go. It wasn't without pain or tears or well wishes, but when we left that night, we both knew it was goodbye for good. When I dropped Drew off at his apartment, he waved goodbye and his six-foot Asian frame walked past the headlights of my car. A peaceful departing of ways, a blessing as we walked our different stories.

When I get the chance, I watch Drew's latest movie and as the credits roll, I wait for his name to flash up against the black screen. The smallest smile comes across my face because there is a deep satisfaction remembering the night we let each other go to pursue our different dreams. I smile, remembering that night at the crowded coffee shop, with strangers speaking in sign language, and how truly listening, truly staying with each other, changed the course of my life.

8

MY FRIEND SAM

An Invitation to Break and Surrender Dreams

Sam and I grew up together, literally two blocks apart. I lived on 1204 Birch Way. If I crossed through a field of knee-high weeds to Alapat Street, passed the pastor's house, turned left onto Rose, and then took a quick right, there was Sam's house, 610 McClain Avenue. He was seven, I was eight when we met. My first memory of him was how his hair stuck straight up as if he literally dumped a bottle of hair gel on the top of his head. I remember when we danced awkwardly in junior high in a multipurpose room smelling of cheap cologne and punch. In high school we breezed in and out of each other's lives: attended dances, camps, and Sunday night Bible studies together. We were nothing more and nothing less than friends. Friends that laughed and had a secret handshake.

In college we went on a river trip and the two of us stayed up half the night, staring at the sky filled with stars. He had always just been Sam—my silly, skinny, tall, ridiculously smart friend, Sam Paschall. It wasn't until we both moved back home after college, just blocks apart, that I ever saw Sam any differently than that.

We both worked with the high school kids at our church as interns, and we commuted to grad school over an hour away together. One evening after a ministry event, we started talking. The fluorescent lights in the parking lot were humming above, casting long shadows down his face. But it wasn't just the shadow from the lights that made me see him for the first time that evening. It was the darkness in his soul he fumbled around trying to articulate that made me see him. He spoke about the same darkness I had felt inside of me. He was the first boy I met who could see the same way I could. Sam wasn't asking me to fix him. He was inviting me to be with him. That was the night I saw him as someone more than just a friend, as a person my soul gravitated toward with ease. It was natural and right, like coming home.

Sam was passionate and well spoken, his hair in tangles down to his shoulders and mostly hidden by an oversized beanie. He only owned secondhand cowboy shirts and always had a satchel draped across his chest. Seeing Sam's pain behind his eloquent speech and salty, beach-matted hair made me feel less alone. It gave me comfort; it gave me a sense of connectedness. It made my soul smile. After that night in the parking lot, we were rarely apart. Almost every day, for hours and hours, we would hang out. When we went to our separate homes, blocks away, we would text and call and continue our conversation until we could barely keep our eyes open. I didn't want to be in a committed relationship. I had been in a long relationship and was broken. The scales-shedding, realities-ripping-me-open, heart-bleeding kind of broken. As much as I loved spending time with Sam, I held him at a distance.

Sam first breached the topic of "us" at the French Bakery. The French Bakery is a local breakfast nook in the heart of our little city. They are the creators of the most delicate, delicious, flaky almond croissants. The walls are all painted dramatic blues, yellows, and purples. One summer morning Sam asked me to meet him there before work. Our table, with one leg slightly shorter than the rest, was on the front patio lining the sidewalk. There was a fidgetiness to his body and several long awkward silences. He began by saying how much the last few months of our friendship had changed him. I felt panic grow with every word. I felt the urge to run, to hide, to not let him see my anxiety. I wanted to be anywhere else but at that table with the wobbly leg. Everything about my life was unbalanced. I was in a state of free fall, finding out who I was and what I wanted to do with my life. The thought of any sort of commitment made me turn ice cold. Now, here, at my favorite bakery, he was asking if he could be my boyfriend. I said no. Our goodbye was as awkward as the table.

That Sunday we loaded buses with 500 high school kids and headed to Hume Lake. I was responsible for all the girls, 250 of them. The camp was filled with kids needing counseling or a new wristband or a bandage for their bruises and broken hearts. I'd listen and love and pray and at moments, I'd glance across the chapel and see Sam doing exactly the same thing: loving kids. To anyone else it would have gone unnoticed, but to me, it was everything. It was Friday now and I felt paralyzed on the floor of my cabin. My roommate for the week walked in and, seeing me half naked and in tears, immediately sat down beside me. Our conversation was brief and beautiful and helped me organize my thoughts. I wrestled with only one question: "Would I let myself love him?" He was pulling away. I had to choose what voice I would listen to: fear or love. My fear of being hurt again was all I heard: "Hide, protect, don't let anyone in." But love whispered, "Trust, let go, let love in." I got dressed. I wore my whitewashed jeans and turquoise zip-up hoodie and headed to dinner, my hair untangled, as was my heart. I knew what I needed to do. Love.

Before I could even sit down, I saw a friend of mine, Josh, and I pulled him aside. I told him I wasn't going to be afraid to love Sam any longer. Josh did something I will never forget. His six-foot-four stature bent down and looked me dead straight in the eyes. He put his hands on my shoulders and practically shook me, saying, "Run. Anjuli, you have to run and tell him right now. Run." I'm not sure if it was the lack of sleep or a flashback to every romantic Meg Ryan movie ever made, but I did, I ran to Sam. Pushing through a sea of students heading from dinner to evening chapel, I frantically scanned the crowd for the tall, long-haired boy I had just decided to love. I ran, heart beating outside of my chest. I had to get to him. I remember praying that if I was meant to talk with Sam, he would be easy to find. I opened the back door to the meeting hall; his face was the first one I saw.

If I were really honest I would have told him that I loved him, kissed him, and asked him to marry me, but let's be honest, I'm no Meg Ryan (although I did try to pull off her messy pixie haircut at least three times before I realized my thick, straight Asian hair just can't do it). I told him I was ready to give us a try. But my words didn't touch him. It was like trying to throw a feather at a fan; my words were blown away. It was as though after our last conversation he shut himself off from me, pulled away, and slammed the door closed. Sam was done. Only days before, he wanted me. He had made himself vulnerable to me and then mentally moved on to protect himself.

Everything began to collapse in on me, the sharp sting of rejection slicing me into the shreds of a girl left cut up and unloved. I felt like unwanted mail, torn and tossed aside. That night I couldn't sleep. I woke up early and walked across camp to breakfast. I saw the lake, wide and open and deep as it always was. But I didn't want to see it. I had to look away. Wide and open and deep only meant I was drowning. The lake water was rising; I was sinking. This pain, the rejection, the way Sam said no and slapped my love back in my face was just a warning of what was already on its way. A storm was coming.

Sam was a symbol of what I thought would bring me absolute happiness. I wanted to be loved, known, and, more than anything, wanted. I wanted a relationship with someone I could come home to and share life with, a soul mate. There was a gnawing tug inside of me. My will against God's. I dug my feet in, begging and pleading for God to give me what I wanted. Demanding it almost. And there was God, unmoved. So I banged against the door harder, and I cried longer. I grew angrier and stomped louder. When I let my righteousness ring my desire to death, a quiet came over me. A stillness as calm as the lake at sunrise. The final option was devastating to accept, the death of my dream. Surrender.

God was inviting me to let go of the one thing I believed would make my life complete. He wanted everything and all of me. Even hope itself has to be given over to God. Hope became a false sense of security for me. It was easier to cling to hope than it was to cling to Jesus. But hope can't save me. It can't change my circumstances; it can't make what is wrong right. I had to release my reason, logic, and sneaky ways of manipulating others and God into getting what I wanted. I had to surrender my will, my dreams, my everything.

My deepest desire had to crack like Mary's alabaster jar at the feet of Jesus. Mary ushered herself into an unwelcome space and the scent of a million dreams dispersed into the room. The aroma of sweet perfume filled the air while men stared in disgust and disapproval. Her love offering was abrasive and misunderstood. But to Jesus it was everything. It wasn't just that she broke a bottle of expensive oil, it's that she broke. She fell down and gave herself over in a posture of love before Him. Mary didn't just coat His ankles with a lovely fragrance, she bent low and presented her body as a balm before Him (John 12).

I could break my most valued treasure at the feet of Jesus. I could bend my body at His feet. But minutes later, my mind was busy at work mentally trying to put the pieces of my life back together. I was fixated on fixing my problem. I was neurotically jamming my shattered alabaster jar back together. Surrender isn't one simple act; it is permanently staying beside Jesus. Every moment, staying in the agonizing grip of letting go. I had to stay with my heart bleeding and dreams crashing and hope dismantling. Surrender is the beginning of a new story. It may not be the story I envisioned, but it is the one I've been entrusted with. It is the one I have been deemed worthy to carry.

My prayer of surrender wasn't passive like a Sunday morning worship song. Prayer became for me a source of life support. I had to stay right there in order to survive. Surrender was actively prying back my fingers and releasing my will to His. In surrender I found that I wasn't really alone. Jesus was there. Dying to my will and my way was being with Jesus, the person who exemplified surrender. In the dying of my will, I found myself in the presence of God. The God who died in the worst way imaginable died because of love, through love, and for His uncontainable love for me. Surrender felt like I was folding up beside Christ in the garden of Gethsemane, begging for another way. Resurrection was coming. I knew it. It might not be the way I always imagined. It might not be the story I would have written, but somehow the way the story ended mattered less than who I was walking my story with.

It wasn't something instant, magical, or bright and flashy, but there was a slow rebuilding within me. A slow stacking of one moment upon the next that brought me back from breaking. Instead of Sam, or the *hope* of being with someone that could love me, God became my center. He became my hope. I knew that without a soul mate or a best friend or someone to walk through life with, without being a mom, or successful, without anything at all—I knew I would ultimately be okay. Really, really okay. When Sam came back into my life and our relationship took new roots months later, I knew it was an entirely undeserved "I love you" gift from God. I knew I wanted to be with Sam, but I knew now that I didn't *need* to be with him. And when we started dating—after breaking each other's hearts—the boy who always lived blocks away became my boyfriend. He wasn't my savior or my hope or my healer—he was just that, my boyfriend. And that was good.

9

WHEN HE PROPOSED

An Invitation to Sit in the Weeds

When Sam proposed the first time, it was in a field of weeds beside the Colorado River in Blythe, Arizona. It was a place that was familiar to us. Blythe, even on its most beautiful day, is still a horrible, horrible place. On average Blythe is 100 degrees with packs of mosquitoes perpetually swarming the water for their next meal. It is truly miserable. But for us, there is something significant about this trapped-in-an-oven, dry, desert land. Something that trumped the hot weather and pesky bugs. It was in Blythe on a college river trip that Sam and I stayed up half the night out under the stars. We didn't really notice time passing; instead we watched the moon moving brighter across the sky and the glowing stars like fierce firecrackers popping in the blackness. It was just us chatting about God and grace and friends and free will. After that night, we both went away back to college, traveled the world, dated other people, and made a million mistakes, but that night is etched into both our brains. It was the night we laughed and talked and watched in wonder at all the glory in the skies. So, years later, when he pulled the car over and rolled out a blanket in a field of dead grass in the most horrible place on earth, I thought he might ask me to marry him.

This proposal wasn't romantic. I remember a few things about that mid-spring day by the river. I remember how much I hated my haircut. I was in the dreadful process of growing out my hair. My thick, short, choppy hair made it look like I was wearing a helmet on my head. It was also noisy. There was a brawl escalating just across the road from us. Tension was rising with the volume of rap music. And it was hot, really, really hot; the bugs were even sweating and sticking to each other. Maybe it was the mere shock of the moment or the gang fight or the sweltering heat, but there was this tiny voice in the back of my head that couldn't believe what was happening. He read a chapter out of *The Alchemist* and said we were twin souls and that he wanted me to be his wife. I remember sitting nearly completely in his lap at this point, arms wrapped around his, thinking *Yes, yes, yes!* Then I looked down at the ring with eyes wide, thinking *No, no, no! This might just be the ugliest ring I've ever seen.* I threw it on my finger and hugged him fiercely, trying to buy myself more time to compose myself and respond to the generous gift he had given me. On the drive home we called our parents and siblings and friends and shared the good news.

I kept staring at my ring in different lights, hoping that a new angle would help me fall in love with it. Something wasn't sitting well with me. I couldn't quite describe it, but the entire drive home I felt uneasy. Like I was the uncomfortable girl alone at a dance club, trying hard to look like she was having a good time, but obviously wasn't. My uneasiness had nothing to do with accepting Sam's proposal and everything to do with his execution and the circumstances surrounding my life at the time.

My family's resistance rang loud in my ears. They believed in engagements after years of dating and not four months of it. I was nervous that they wouldn't take us seriously. I feared what people would think. I worried that I'd have to wear this ugly ring my entire life and about my awful haircut. The way I had envisioned being proposed to never included a desert, bugs, and wearing my sister's Urban Outfitters faded pink T-shirt.

The night turned more uncomfortable when we arrived at my parents' house, where a surprise party was waiting. Somehow Sam neglected to communicate to my parents that he had invited nearly fifty people over to their house. Quite literally, everyone was surprised. An intimate evening that my parents and sisters catered for a party of nine turned into scrambling for paper cups and raiding the pantry for any available snacks to throw out on the table. It was a feast of crackers, nuts, and water. My parents were gracious and welcomed the horde of unexpected (but loved) guests into their home. When we arrived, everyone hugged us and took pictures and begged us to tell them how he asked. When the last guests had left and Sam and I were alone, I told him the truth about the ugly ring. He promised we could return it and find the perfect one.

It took several days of difficult conversations to express that I was so excited to marry him, but that my vision of the "will you marry me" moment had always looked something like a beautiful black dress and roses and candles and painted fingernails. So when the new ring arrived, he asked if he could ask me again. This time I wore a black and white skirt with elephants lining the rim, a slim black lace top and cardigan, with sparkling black flats. Sam arrived at my door with flowers, and my mom was there snapping pictures like the paparazzi. He took me out to the most expensive restaurant I've ever eaten at, where we sat at a reserved table in arms' reach of the ocean. We drove downtown. He put a blindfold over my eyes. Guiding me through the streets of San Diego, he took me up in a tiny elevator and told me to wait. Blinded and cold and curious, I heard the buzz of the street below. We were on the top of a building. When I opened my eyes, there were candles everywhere. Sam sat me down in a chair and read to me out of the book of Ruth. A story of friendship between Naomi and her daughter-in-law Ruth; "Where you go, I will go." With that, he knelt beside me, slipped the most delicate ring on my finger, and asked me to marry him— for the second time.

Nearly fifteen years into marriage and five kids later, I laugh thinking about how I made Sam propose twice. I love telling the story of how he proposed in a desert trailer park the first time, bought me an ugly ring, and surprised my parents by throwing a surprise party at their house. Most of the time, I never tell people how he proposed the second time. I probably only tell the first story of his sudden proposal in a field of weeds because it is the one that is most dear to me, the way he stumbled and tried and everything turned out upside down. After fifteen years of marriage, I realize that most of the time we are walking through the wilderness and doing our best to hold on to each other along the way, in the dark, dry, and sometimes difficult long years of desert. Marriage is so much more about being with someone than it is about being worshiped by them.

For us, marriage has had so many beautiful moments—like the night Sam baked me a dozen pies for my birthday party and decorated our patio with Christmas lights in July. There was the time he serenaded me on my thirtieth birthday. He practiced for hours with my sisters and brother-in-law and when I least expected it, my non-musical and tone-deaf husband turned on a microphone and sang to me under the stars and in front of my favorite people. Sometimes he comes home from work with a lovely bouquet of orange flowers and insists I sit on the couch as he manhandles bath- and bedtime on his own. On our eighth anniversary he bought me an electric blanket (something I believe to be one of man's greatest inventions behind the dishwasher, flat iron, and those ice machines that make chewable ice). The moments we held each of our five babies for the first time. There have been so many moments that felt like I was in heaven, but so many more are mundane ones.

Marriage is about endurance and hard sacrifices and slow personal deaths. So much of life is learning how to live in the desert, where water is limited: growing and trusting and grieving and dying in the thorns and bristles of browned grass. For us, it has been about trudging through debt and getting swallowed up in it again. It has been about broken cars and break-ins. About impulsive decisions that we paid steep, drawn-out prices for and saying yes when we really should have said no. It has been about surprise pregnancies and career changes. It has been about surviving seven years of grad school and the rejection of churches we loved. For us, marriage has been about overflowing toilets, leaky faucets, and aimlessly following around a toddler. It has been about crying babies and cars refusing to start. Marriage has been about walking with Sam through his parents' divorce: his dad leaving, his mom staying, and his brother moving in with us. Marriage has been about negative pregnancy tests, emergency C-sections, dangerously ill children, and weeks without sex.

It is about so many trips to Target that inevitably drain our bank account, reminders to pay the landscaper and pick up laundry detergent and go through the endless stacks of mail. Marriage is the hard work of turning to each other instead of the next episode on Netflix. It is the battle of not letting stress and conflicting schedules and cranky children pull us away from each other, but toward each other. So much of marriage is wading through the dark patches and waiting for light to break.

Because our marriage isn't best when we are on a date night, dishes done, or our love languages fulfilled. Our marriage isn't best when we have the kids composed, renovation projects completed, and finances figured out. No, our marriage isn't even best when we listen, laugh, or spend evenings awake whispering about our dreams. I know our marriage is healthiest when we are honest, when we confess, and when we stay in our weeds. When we vulnerably crack open our hearts and let the other one peek in, I know we are moving toward growth. Our marriage is gaining muscles when I tell him how I still struggle with pride, resentment, anxiety, and regret. When we talk about what's really going on, our weaknesses, like water, pour hope into our loneliness. The soil surrounding all of who we are grows more resilient. Roots reaching down deeper and longer, wider and stronger, gripping earth as a mighty force.

Letting Sam stay in my weeds has been excruciating at times. Letting him come close has meant breaking through thick walls and working through my manipulative tactics to keep him out. There are few people in my life who I don't have to be something for, to be loved in return. Most relationships require me to keep the conversation going, have something valuable to offer, or meet another's needs. I think this is true of how I relate to God as well.

I've been a Christian most of my life. Honestly, my prayer life is embarrassing for someone who has walked with God since she has barely been walking. I don't talk about my inner prayer life very much. My dialogue with God can feel chillingly quiet, one-sided, and dry at times. Of course, this makes me feel guilty. When I pray out loud, I feel even more awkward. My words are clunky and come out all wrong. I wish I could say I pray constantly and my conversations with Jesus are eloquent and intimate. But it's not that way.

Oftentimes I catch myself talking to God like I talk to my dad. I'm trying to get it right, not mess up, and avoid conflict. It's complicated. I present a picture of who I think I should be instead of who I actually am. I want God to see the lovely, strong, "see how good I'm doing" me. Sometimes I go all day or days without praying at all. Then all of a sudden, I shake myself awake from my numb state of living and try to make up for my spiritual mistakes. I have a tendency to beat myself up into doing better. I come back to God, praying like I need to get back on His good side again. Many of my prayers are motivated by shame, not love. But prayer isn't about doing another "thing." Maybe it's a lot more like how it is with Sam, me, and the weeds.

I'm messy. But messy doesn't equal bad. These are just my weeds. I have lots of them. I'm learning not to pick them before I let God and Sam in. I'm tempted to pull out the weed whacker, but instead, I wait. My relationship with God and Sam and people I love most in the world is about learning the sacred art of presence. I'm letting them be with me. I'm learning to let God roam the boring, lush, confusing, cluttered, and unattended long stretches of land inside of me. And it is hard to not clean up first. Painful actually. I want it all organized and landscaped and sculpted. I want to offer people a better, improved, I'm-worthy-of-your-love me. But I let the weeds stay and I let others in. I ask the question, "How have my actions negatively affected you?" I want them to be a mirror for my soul. "Can you please help me see things about myself that I can't see?" I let them love the true me. Love is not possible without confession. Love requires honesty. There is no other greater sense of love than being accepted in my wild, unstructured, and tangled insides.

God is on the mission of creating a culture inside of me where I welcome love into my middle. I'm not fully at a place where

I'm comfortable with others strolling about in my mess. But I'm more aware than ever of what it feels like when I try to clear out the landscape before letting Jesus and others in. I feel panicky and my nervous eyes scan the room for exit signs. I create stories where I convince myself that I'm too much for people to handle. I reject them before they could ever reject me. I'm tempted to lie and distract their attention and pretend everything is just fine.

But I'm learning to lay down my shears. I don't want to prune or control the pathways anymore. I let God do the sacred work of transforming my soul, cutting back the branches, and pruning the bushes. That's His holy work. And when I pray with words, I let them be imperfect, infrequent, muddled, and child-like. I can pray with tears, silence, half smiles, and by taking a nap. I can pray with anger, watching the sky change colors, scrolling through Instagram, and while packing lunches. I think God is delighted when I stay with Him as I am. Regular life with Jesus can be just that: regular. There are fewer mountaintops and valleys than there are just long stretches of everyday life. This prayer language is a new one I'm still learning. This love dialect requires a lot of one thing: grace. I need heaps of grace to remember I am loved in the middle of my messy, ordinary life. So I'm drinking in grace. Getting drunk on it, really.

After nearly fifteen years, Sam's first proposal has become my favorite. These weeds are my teacher. It's a classroom of unconditional acceptance and loyalty. Weeds teach me how to be loved. Truly loved. Asking me to marry him in a field of weeds was an incredibly accurate picture of what our lives would come to look like. So often I feel the pressure to get ahead, move faster, and arrive sooner at some imaginary line of marriage or my faith, yet I'm continuously brought back here, to my weeds. As much as I want to escape the chokehold the twines have on me, those places that repeatedly entangle me, I'm learning that when I sit with Sam and God there, we are bonded. There is true intimacy.

When I remember that hot day, with my bushy haircut and the gang fight brawling in the background and the ugly ring, I wouldn't change it for all the world because it was a part of what made us, us (well, maybe just the ring). I never knew anything beautiful could be birthed out of a place called Blythe, but something was. We were, weeds and all.

Marriage is so much more about being with someone than it is about being worshiped by them.

10

547 EAST 6TH AVE

An Invitation to Hurt for Home

S am called me midafternoon, announcing, "We got the place!" We were four months out from getting married. The most exciting part wasn't the wedding or honeymoon, but actually making a home together. I looked forward to decorating walls, filling the kitchen cabinets with clean wedding dishes, and planting a garden. We didn't want something commercial or cookie cutter. We wanted something with character, so we drove up and down the streets of old Escondido scoping out "for rent" signs. One afternoon my mom mentioned she might have a connection for us. She knew a widower who lived downtown, and the flat above his house just became vacant. His name was John Gorbet. We would come to call him Papa John.

Papa John was older. He had tennis balls attached to his walker and could fall asleep in any position. His back was bent with years of hard work. He used an old wire hanger to help him button his Hawaiian shirts, and he could MacGyver any mechanical mishap. He had a story for everything. I think I heard the story about his bus getting stuck on a mission trip in Mexico more times than I can count; it got better every time. He served in World War II and was stationed in the South Pacific on land and on sea. He told us stories about the night they were attacked by kamikaze pilots right in front of his boat and how he watched a deceased pilot's goggles float to the surface of the water. He told these stories as if they were still happening, unfolding before his eyes. The stars, glowing like hope in the tar-like blackness of night, were still fresh to him, and he told how, even in darkness, no one ever really slept during the war.

Papa John's body was frail, but this was not a man to be messed with. He tended to his plot of land with pride and resilience. When friends of ours were spending well over $1,000 for a small studio apartment, Papa John charged us $200 for a 900-square-foot flat. $200 and trash duties. The flat had one full bedroom, which I painted a deep red. A full-sized bathroom with an original claw-foot bathtub and linoleum floors that were impossible to keep clean. The kitchen had a max capacity of one (and that person better be short and skinny, or they wouldn't fit). All the doorways were small, and Sam was constantly ducking his head in and out of rooms. Each room had the most hideous green carpet with stains telling stories from past tenants. The place was tiny;

some of the windows had cracks. It had creaky floors and the occasional unwanted rodent, but the place was perfect because it was ours. We shared our first few years of marriage living above Papa John, and every night we fell asleep to the sound of him wheezing in pain.

We were poor. Poorer than poor. I remember sorting out our wedding gifts—there was a pile for the gifts we could return to get cash back, and we did. We returned towels so we could pay our $200 rent. Sam was working as a driver for his dad's plumbing company, and I worked at a high school correctional center, jobs we both disliked. We were both finishing our graduate degrees and commuting to LA twice a week. We were so broke we budgeted ourselves one trip to Starbucks a week: Wednesday mornings. I loved Wednesday mornings when I could sip on my extra hot, no-water chai tea latte. We ate and did laundry at our parents' houses. We had no clue what living on our own and completely supporting ourselves really meant. Entering marriage, we both knew what the thin envelope in the mail from your bank meant: overdraft. We had loans and debt and maxed-out credit cards. Words like *taxes* and *savings* made our heart rates rise. *Retirement* and *401k* sounded more like Arabic and induced a glazed-over stare.

Our first Christmas we splurged and bought Amy Grant's Christmas album *A Tender Tennessee Christmas*. I was so giddy as we drove around our little city listening to holiday songs on repeat. I'll never forget our first tree standing small in our corner, twinkling, and dressed with my parents' leftover ornaments and a ribbon from our wedding table decor. I'll always remember when I unwrapped a little black box. Tucked in the black velvet was a wedding band, the one we were unable to afford a few months earlier when we exchanged vows. It was thin and small and diamond-less but sat flush perfectly against my engagement ring. Being poor makes you depend and trust and really pray. And we prayed desperately for a way through.

Being without a steady income, grappling with debt, and still in school, we did the most practical thing next. We had a baby. We had only been married eight months. We were young and naïve and didn't always think things through. Our conversation went a little like this: "Should we start trying to have a baby?" He shrugged and answered, "Sure." We were so stupid and reckless. Who plans to start a family by shrugging their shoulders? Stupid people do. Lucky for us, God is totally into stupid people.

It wasn't the most ideal situation to bring a baby into, but our 1906 home perched at the corner of Grape and 7th Street holds some of my favorite memories. We learned to fight in that small flat, how to resolve disagreements, how to make our favorite Korean cucumber salad. We learned how to walk the tightrope from dating to married to parenting in that place. We had Manoah; two years later we had Samuel. The summer after Sammy was born, our little flat felt like a furnace, but the boys giggled and played for hours in the water hose. We would sleep in on Saturdays and skip church on Sundays. It was bliss.

In an odd way, I miss it. I miss staring into our fridge wondering how to make a meal out of eggs, a chicken breast, and wilted lettuce. I miss living simply and praying hard for the basic necessities in life. We had so little, but so much. Hearing Papa John's walker shuffling just below our floors, with his furnace always ablaze, was a constant reminder of God's provision on our lives. Every time we wrote that $200 check we exhaled with awe that we could be there, in this tiny haven, paying a rent we could barely afford with enough food to eat and with the perfect amount of diapers to get us through the day.

Papa John died when he was 89 years old. We lived at 547 East 6th Avenue for four years. It feels like yesterday that I played with Manoah in the front yard. Papa John sat in his rocking chair on his deck, watching us and the day unfold. He gained nothing from us. We rarely took out the trash on time, and our babies cried loudly, and our parties went late into the night. He gave us grace when he could have given us late fees. He was a channel of God's generosity toward us. He gave us a taste of home.

Home is a place I've always been searching for. Home for me growing up smelled like fresh bread and honeysuckle. It tasted like sweetened condensed milk poured over morning pancakes, fresh-squeezed orange juice on spring afternoons, and sour grass all summer long. Home meant a foyer filled with a hundred sandals, the spicy hot smell of curry, card games till midnight, and my mom tuning her violin and heart to find pitch and peace. Home was laced with the sounds of sisters singing and strangers camped out and snoring on the living room floor. Home felt like fake falling asleep so the slender arms of my Asian father would carry me up our creaky, attic-like stairs and unfold me into bed. I never felt as wanted or safe or loved as I did when he carried me with my eyes closed and chin tucked into his chest.

Home also meant steadily reading body language and managing explosive rage with my do-good behavior. It meant hiding out in my room until all the screaming stopped. I was good at pretending nothing was wrong. But there were wrongs we never spoke of. There were broken things I tried to mend with wit, playfulness, and my pretty face. I can trace my heritage and history and see sins passed down from one generation to the next like eye color and dimples. Sins like shame, favoritism, abandonment, and anger. I am Asian American. And though I didn't overtly experience racism growing up, I did live and breathe and carry on the cultural sins from my parents, their parents, and probably the parents before them. Sins I might—but pray I don't—pass down to my kids. If I sit with the tragic and tender map of my family tree I might just weep for days. The broken promises, the forgotten children, the marriages forged in lies, pain, and silence might just be the end of me. My home was good, but also confusing. And the older I get, the more I realize how layered and thick and complicated it all really was. I realize that these splinters in my story find resolve when I invite the wrongs and rights to reconcile. As I try to understand my home growing up, it doesn't all get better, but a deep sense of acceptance emerges. The hard and the holy don't jab at each other, but join hands. Wholeness is awakened.

I hurt for home. I ache for it, really. I long for true exhale. I've searched for home in significance, relationships, status, and skin tone. I've looked for my home in boys who would love me, friends who would want me, a husband to know me, people to admire me, and children to obey me. And yet, the ache for home aches all the more. Every home I've put my hope in has yet to fill the deepest longings of my soul. I've always heard that home isn't a place, but the people you are with. But I think it's more than that. I think it is a place and people and peace. It is a shared language, overflowing joy, perfect justice, extended grace, and forever love. I think home is all the things we desire most in life but haven't fully experienced. As Tim Keller preached, "You're actually looking for a song you remember but you have never heard."[1] We know home, even though we don't fully *know* home.

This never-ending hurt for home is down there, deep inside of me. Even when life is falling gracefully as I hoped it would, the ache persists. Sometimes it is loud. Sometimes it is quiet. My hunger for home is always there. But instead of filling my ache with food, social media, or shopping, I'm feeling it, staying with it. Because when something inside of me feels empty the temptation will always be to fill it. Loneliness isn't to be feared, pushed aside, or pressed under, but invited out. I feel its ferocious appetite and the ways I'm tempted to stuff my void with anything and everything but God. Instead of begging for belonging in a world where my skin color and culture isn't common, I'm naming and feeling my longing: "Yes, there it is again . . . my hurt for home." I'm accepting it as part of my human condition to crave a home that doesn't entirely exist in this time zone. C. S. Lewis describes it perfectly: "If I find in myself a desire which no experience in this world can satisfy, the most probable explanation is that I was made for another world."[2] I'm learning to pray through my ache and accept that it will always be a limp I live with. A limp we all have to stay with this side of heaven.

When Papa John let us stay with him, his home became a placeholder. It held us safe in place of heaven. He showed us that life is to be given and shared with long sips of tea and storytelling at its finest. Without his kindness, we never would have survived those first few years of marriage and grad school and babies. He gave these young newlywed wanderers a home with cracks in the walls and hobbit-sized rooms, a place to lay our foundation.

I believe we all can be placeholders of heaven for others. We can create a seat at a table, offer a single cup of coffee, leave bread on a doorstep, or clear an hour in our schedule. God will continually bring us people who are desperately in need of home. If we can embrace each other's differences, move toward the disabled, welcome the foreigner, laugh with a child, talk with the elderly, all kinds of heaven can burst open like a flower in bloom here on earth. Even the tiniest spaces can become a place for others to taste eternity.

I've lived in several different homes. Each home represents a different placeholder in my life. There was my childhood home that functioned more like a hostel, the house on East 6th Avenue, the green house that held our enormous grief like a golden goblet. We lived in the brown house with the crickets and huge strokes of healing. There was the Poway house with the single fruit tree in our front yard and heaps of sadness. The hand-sized lemons drooped heavy like teardrops, putting my loneliness on display for all the neighbors to see. Our current home has brick pathways and bay windows and lots of babies. Houses aren't just walls. Papa John taught me that they can be placeholders for what we long for most in this world—home.

11

SHOWING UP

An Invitation to See

I've always liked taking pictures. I love the energy between subject and artist. I love the magic, light, beauty, and love seen through a lens. While my baby slept, I often found myself on photography blogs. Eventually, I emailed my wedding photographer with loads of questions and made appointments with a few friends who owned nice cameras to pick their brains.

Then I did one of the scariest things in my life. I bought a camera. Not just any camera, but a good one, an expensive one, one that took a real camera battery and not just AAs. Sam went with me. He made the purchase while I paced back and forth bashfully behind him. I went home with my big black camera and didn't touch it for days. Even the box scared me. Every time I saw it, I felt intimidated, insecure, and insane for having the audacious dream of being a photographer. I was afraid of being judged. I was afraid of not being able to understand the camera manual and not being able to figure out what all those little buttons meant. I was terrified of failing and completely embarrassed to even admit that I wanted to be a photographer.

I took pictures for free. I wasn't great, but I was learning. I shopped on Craigslist for cheap equipment and I started a blog. I sent emails asking questions to strangers and stalked online a handful of photographers that I loved. The more pictures I took, the more I obsessed over it. I was shocked every time someone signed up for a session and terrified to ask for money in exchange. I shot my first wedding when I was nine months pregnant with Samuel. The year I officially launched my business, I shot nearly thirty weddings. I felt more confident behind a camera, but the looming feeling of failure wasn't going away. I was being published on blogs and featured in wedding magazines, but I still couldn't call myself a photographer. Instead, I always said, "I like taking pictures," when people asked me what I did for a living. Even with all the inquiries and contracts and rave reviews, something in me still felt miserably small.

Success felt like something for a limited few, and I had to work hard to get my share of it. I was always comparing myself to other photographers, always beating myself up, always needing people's approval, always needing more bookings. I felt like I was behind, like I needed to be doing more: buying gear more, updating my Facebook status more, redefining my online presence more, sending birthday cards to brides more, and signing up for the next hippest photography seminar more. I needed to be more of everything in order to be successful or accomplished at anything. The dark chorus of voices screaming at me that I wasn't enough only seemed to get louder as I added more. I exhausted myself with posting, blogging, and strapping myself to my computer for hours at a time. I became obsessed with making my business more of a success.

I'll never forget the night I sat down with Sam and pleaded with him to reassure me that my photography was good enough. We had these conversations frequently. I would ramble on for hours about how I was failing. I clung to every comment, critique, compliment, always in a constant state of comparison. Every conversation was like twisting a towel—wringing out all the water, squeezing out the very last drop—hoping this time there was a magical word he could say that would satisfy my need for approval. But there was no magic, no key phrase that lifted me from my own battle with failure.

That night Sam said there was nothing he could say to make me feel okay. No amount of publicity or publications, no number of features or followers would ever be enough to give me worth. I had to accept that failure or success wasn't something I could gain or lose. It wasn't an object to obtain. Those categories had to be eliminated entirely. No amount of getting, accomplishing, or achieving will ever satisfy the soul. The soul focused on gaining power, influence, and admiration will only grow hungrier. The soul satisfied will be still. It will be free. The real question wasn't am I successful or failing, but am I walking in faith? Faith to move forward and faith to accept my gifts as offerings to the world around me. Do I trust that I can be me and let God do the rest?

Success, for me, took on an entirely new meaning. It became less about numbers, comments, and a business plan and more about shooting purely, capturing movement, and helping people feel beautiful. I stopped stressing about getting praise from the right people and making my name known. I decided to just show up, simply me. Me, with my whole personality, my navy blue camera bag, and my ability to capture love the only way I knew how. Success shifted from the pressure to constantly network and climb some sort of invisible ladder. I measured success by how well I offered people love through the art of a clicking camera. If I could walk away from a shoot knowing I showed up in faith, gave myself in love, and kindly shared my artful images with others, I was a success. Period.

I started to see people not for what they could do to advance my career, but as sojourners on this rugged journey of life together. I saw mothers stroking their daughters' hair. Fathers hiding in bedrooms, writing toasts, and weeping when they walked their daughters down the aisle. I found the aged hands of grandparents and the toes of infants in pink gowns. I've witnessed the most inappropriate garter tosses. I've melted in awe of first dances that ended with husband and wife heaped over each other in tears. The moment I start to feel anxiety I realize it's because I'm trying to be something or someone other than who I am. Anxiety is always an indicator that I am trying to control the uncontrollable. When I walk in the doors of a hotel room or home filled with strangers, if I show up just as me, Anjuli, I do just fine. Clear heart. Crisp vision.

Photography has taken me around the world, across oceans, and throughout America. It has taken me inside the stories of births and deaths and lifelong commitments. Photography has introduced me to cultures and languages. I've shot $100,000 weddings and $50 weddings. I've shot weddings on boats, in zoos, in barns, and in backyards. I've shot weddings in the wide-open acres of a Georgia field and at a New York estate with trees towering over the reception. I've dodged traffic in downtown San Francisco and Tokyo. I've chased the late-summer sunlight in Seattle. I've had my legs chomped on by vicious Idaho mosquitoes and been stung by bees in rural lavender fields in order to get the perfect shot.

Oftentimes people approach me who want to pursue a career in photography. I tell them immediately I'm the worst person to come to if they want a strategy on how to build a business. My business model is built on love, and that won't always make you rich. But if they want to follow a dream, then I ask them to grab coffee. We all have one calling. One deep, right, true, foundational calling in life—to love God and to love others. It's really that easy, but really just that hard. This one calling permeates all of life and ought to motivate all of what we do. Love is always the business plan and always the answer. Your gifts, dreams, bents, personality, and natural abilities all function as a means to accomplish that one and only purpose in life.

God has a masterful way of doing things backwards. When the world pulls me toward popularity, power, and prestige, God says, "Get smaller, let go of control, surrender significance." The world pressures me to be the first, get in the spotlight, and be strong. But

God teaches that the way to true life is different — be last, shine the light on Him, and live painfully close to my weaknesses. Learning to see God is learning to see the world through an upside-down lens. If I want to see Jesus, I will find Him where I least expect. I will find Him hanging out with unpopular people or doing mundane, ordinary work. He will be with the small, sick, and shameful. He will be washing the feet of the doubtful and deceitful. He welcomes those just trying to figure it out, faithless and failing, those who forget to pray, and those who pray poetically.

When I look around me and anxiety makes me angry because other people are doing things better, faster, and bigger, I am drawn back to the way God works. I am invited back to this upside-down way of seeing. When stress mounts up, when I obsess about being seen by a certain person on social media, at church, or in my line of work, I am invited back to the most unexpected and common place — the table. At the communion table, I see right into God and He sees right into me. The place where Jesus served the betrayer and the eager, the prideful and the poor. Jesus held out physical nourishment to Judas, who would double-cross Him, and Peter, who would deny Him. He saw right into their past, present, and future and served them anyway. Hidden in ordinary wine and ordinary bread, I see Jesus inviting my fragile and fractured places back to Him and the story He is writing just for me. My single, divine, God-ordained story is wrapped up into His story. I remember who I am, where I've come from, and the beauty He sees in me. All my dismembered parts come back together through sip and savor. I make peace with myself and God makes peace with me here. The never-enough, hurried, and insecure parts of me find rest when I remember and I am re-membered at the table. If Jesus can serve Judas, I have to believe He can serve me as well.

Jesus is always on the move toward my wholeness. So, I stay. I stay here with my confession, panic, and desperate need for approval. Christ, at the table, stays with me. His eyes are on me. I am seen with my drive for advancement, selfish ambition, and fear of insignificance. He passes me nourishment for my body and for my soul. Jesus brings me back to my worthiness and constant welcome. His stance stays the same no matter what the condition of my heart may be. At the table, God is always offering me a way out of my neurotic need to be seen by offering me a way into relationship with Him. I want to see myself, God, and others from this place. I want to show up to my life from a posture of being seen.

I don't want to show up with my gifts in order to be seen. I want to show up because I am seen. I spent a lot of my life showing up just so I could be noticed. I needed the affirmation of others to feel secure inside. It is such an exhausting way to live. I used the validating eyes of everyone else to feel worthy. But at the table God sees me. When I am seen by Him, I don't need the wink and smile of anyone else. Here, I am free. Free to be who I am without the fear of judgment, criticism, or will-they-still-like-me anxiety.

Being seen by God propels me to see others. I am compelled to show up and use my gifts as an offering of love. So much of life is about showing up. Show up for the difficult conversations, speak my voice, listen, and extend myself to them in love. Show up to the job interview, apply for a business license, make the call, end the relationship, own my ideas, make another meal, and do not back down or away. I am learning to be the mom and photographer and friend that only I can be; not the person next to me, not the superwoman icons on social media, not the leaders in the industry, but me. Simple, profound, unique, lovely: the one and only me.

At the end of my five minutes on this incredible earth, I hope I haven't squandered the gifts I have been given. I hope that I didn't buy in to the lie that success and failure are tied to a number or platform or specific outcome. I pray I stay with my dreams even when I am afraid of failure. I desperately want God to make something lovely out of my life. Something really beautiful. It's really just five minutes I've been given, maybe eight, and I don't want to miss it because I was too nervous to walk on water or see God do miracles with my mess. I want to see life through an eternal lens of being seen.

It may seem paradoxical, backwards, and upside down, but I refuse to measure success by what I can see on this side of things. I have to wait until I meet Jesus face-to-face. And when I arrive at forever, I hope to hear Him say, "Well done, my good and faithful one." This is success. So I'm gonna keep showing up and when strangers ask what I do, with my gaze steady and a slight smile, I'll say, "I'm a photographer."

The soul focused on gaining power, influence, and admiration will only grow hungrier. The soul satisfied will be still. It will be free.

12

GLOW

An Invitation to Fear

My friend Maria glows. I'm not sure if it's the way she dresses—her Mexican-infused sense of fashion, perfectly pulling off loud floral-printed shirts with pink shorts and platforms—or her sassy personality and laugh that commands the room's attention. She just has it, a glow. I've known Maria since college. I remember meeting her at our church's college group, the gorgeous mocha-colored girl; she was hard to miss.

Maria and I were pregnant with our first babies together. She gave birth to little Gali girl two weeks after my Manoah was born. We cried together, went on walks together, and, together, survived the newborn phase. Maria's bluntness and boldness always gave me space to speak freely and honestly about just how challenging having a baby was. I never felt like I had to hide my feelings of failure or frustration with her. The truth was, she never held back about how much she struggled with her all-nighters with Gali and how much she missed working and how being a stay-at-home mom really sucked at times.

It is so refreshing to meet someone honest. It feels like brushing your teeth or throwing open the windows on a stuffy day or freshly cut cold watermelon on a summer afternoon, just amazing. A sure sign I feel free with someone is whether or not I pick up my home before they come over. Some people make me panic when I know they are swinging by; I frantically run about the house jamming things into drawers and cramming closets shut. But when Maria comes over, I don't hustle to clean. I feel free to let her walk into my mess without fear of judgment, without needing to impress or make excuses. Some people have the power to set others at ease. That's what Maria does; she sets me at ease.

Maria and her husband, Dan, adopted two children from Rwanda. They went from having just Gali to having three kids under the age of four, two of whom didn't speak English. It was a tough transition. I remember Maria coming over after she came back from Africa and just after we had bought a house. She brought a pineapple, and Starbucks, and a housewarming gift. I sliced the pineapple as we talked about Africa and what color to paint my walls. While the kids climbed all over each other, we sipped tea and ate pineapple until our tongues started stinging. We encouraged each other to carry on, to get up every morning and take care of ourselves in the midst of the chaos. She drove away with her life packed into a minivan.

I watched her with complete amazement. Even in the emotional, physical, and financial difficulties she faced, Maria still had a glow about her. She still seemed stable and centered and strong. I finally asked Maria about her glow. She answered, "glitter." She went on to inform me that after applying her bright blush she swooshes powdered glitter on her cheekbones. Glitter. That's it? I must have asked her a dozen times . . . glitter? Seriously??

Maria can get away with very rosy cheeks and wearing deep red lipstick. If I wear red lipstick I look like a clown. Not just a clown, but a creepy, Asian-looking clown. Not a geisha beauty, but a clown. I know red lipstick is a mistake, but I could buy glitter. I could sneak in an extra stroke of blush and splash some glitter on my cheeks. Then, I could have the Maria glow too. So I did what any reasonable person does and found myself the exact same MAC glitter product as Maria, with high hopes that my skin and soul would glow as beautifully as hers.

On one of our Tuesday playdates, I asked Maria what she was afraid of. She replied, "Frogs." I rephrased the question, laughing a little, because she obviously didn't understand my question. "No, what are you *most* afraid of in life?" Her response, in all seriousness, was the same: "frogs." Then it clicked, Maria's glow. Her glow had everything to do with how she experiences fear.

Maria battled through poverty. Being born across the border, she survived on street tacos and on dirt floors. Her mom worked two jobs and her dad died in a drug deal. Maria rose above loss, pain, and the worst possible situation. It made her strong. She walked through rock bottom with Jesus and sees the world differently. Maria embraces her story, hard and holy, and sees the world through the lens in which God sees her. Fear doesn't knock Maria down. She feeds her fear with love.

I feed my fear with fear. When fear pops up, I defend or attack it. I feed my fear with Google searches, worst-case scenarios, WebMD, and *Dateline*. I constantly fear "the bad thing" happening one day in my life. I fear pain, emotional separation, or being controlled by others. I fear Sam dying and my kids getting hurt or not following Jesus. I fear not being good enough or letting people down. I worry about a shooter walking into our church sanctuary. I don't like surprises or when the weather changes unexpectedly. I have a fear of rodents and plane crashes and the sounds outside my window. My anxiety churns over in my stomach like a wave tumbling and toppling on the shore. When I look at God, others, or myself with eyes of fear, my only responses are to flee, fight, or freeze. I am always in a stance of defense or attack. I rarely feed my fear with the promises that God is deeply abiding with me, loving me, no matter what the circumstances are. I don't dwell on the truth of God's provision over my life and my loved ones. But when I see the world with eyes of love, everything is a request for or an offer of love. Love transforms everything into a gift to give or to receive.

Fear poured into fear only produces more fear. But love poured into fear awakens me to freedom. At the table of my soul are many voices. Some voices scream, while others are hushed. Some of the voices are kind, slow, and observant; others are suspicious, harsh, incriminating, and mean. Most of my life I've let the loud-est voices have the most power. Voices of people who don't like me, fear, responsibility, sadness, critical, and self-hating voices are really loud at my table. Quiet voices are grace, anger, love, doubt, confidence, and forgiveness. My fear voice has been so loud for so long, and I've fed it with more fear. It's like my voices of fear and distrust huddle at one end of the table, scheming something awful into happening.

But not anymore. I'm taking the mic back. It's not good for my soul to let fear have the final say. I'm learning a new way. Instead of the loudest voices dominating my thoughts, I'm learning to let Jesus and I co-lead the conversation. Every emotion is welcome at the table of my soul, even the most uncomfortable ones. But no one takes over being the boss. No single voice dominates, pushes, or murders another voice. Jesus always gets veto power. He sees the whole picture, my entire purpose, and the path I'm being led on. All the other voices have a secret motive or are shortsighted. God's perspective isn't bound by time and space, but by eternity. He is the One guiding the conversation; His voice is the only one that feeds me with love. Every voice is met with love. At the table of my soul, God draws me back together. All of me is welcome, whole, and at home. When I stay with all of me at the table, the war within me settles.

Maria's glow isn't just from glitter; it's because she isn't tangled up in fear. I see Maria's fearlessness in the way she moves through life with her heart anchored and spirit alive. At the table of her soul, there isn't a battle. There is peace. Fear is in its proper place, and love is at the center. Fear doesn't have power over her. I don't meet up with Maria often. Sometimes I see her on Tuesdays at the farmers' market, where we juggle flowers, fruit, and popcorn and manage children in strollers, wheels hitting curbs and heels. I don't see her much, but I think of her often, every morning, in fact. Every morning when I frost my cheeks with glitter, I think about Maria. I stroke a little extra blush on my cheekbones because everyone needs a little more warmth on their skin, and I gently pat my brush in the glitter. I swoop it across my cheeks. I watch the excess float off and up into the brilliant light streaming in through my bathroom window. I smile. I invite fear to stay at the table of my soul, but not to overpower it. I listen to it, acknowledge it, and let Jesus's voice calm it. Fear dusted with the glitter of love is the only way it dissolves. Love is the only medication that melts it. I think about how Maria's glow makes me want to grab on to love, to drink it and consume it and devour it—merging it into my story until the shine makes my soul dance like hers and the glitter dancing in my bathroom. I see how love brings an effortless, stunning, internal light. Well, that and a little splash of glitter high across my cheekbones.

SUSHI AND

FRIDAY NIGHT LIGHTS

An Invitation to Be Embarrassed

W hen I look back on my short life I see a lengthy list of embarrassing moments that got me to where I am today. In middle school I helped my friend make posters as she ran for school secretary. I convinced her that it was spelled "secratery," and the posters quickly landed us in the not-cool category for the rest of the year. In case you're wondering, she didn't win. I barely scraped by in my classes, doing homework minutes before it was due and getting consistent Cs on every test, retaking Algebra II twice. I tried out for the track team and sprained my ankle the first day. I tried out for water polo and almost drowned.

I was involved in spirit days but somehow always managed to flip around the days, dressing up as a nerd on career day or a twin on Hawaiian shirt day. I was made fun of for my faith and for being on the flag team.

I applied to two colleges and was rejected by one. In college, I managed to skim by in my classes by reading Cliffs Notes in chapel and sneaking into study groups with the smart kids. I am the very reason smart kids don't like group projects. I "quit" my job at Jamba Juice (five minutes before they were about to fire me). I stumbled into grad school. I never turned in homework on time and missed exams entirely. I've broken hearts and hurt people by not returning phone calls and not showing up for the important things like weddings and babies. I completely forgot my sister's birthday one year. I'm terrible at thank-you cards and birthday presents, and I flake on a lot of the commitments I make. My kids wear mismatched shoes and socks every day.

I feel like I'm a constant failure and disappointment to others and myself. No amount of good deeds can take away the ickiness of my disappointment the same way dumping a gallon of hand sanitizer on me can't take away the dirtiness I feel after my kids play in one of those fast-food indoor playgrounds. And, yes, my kids frequently eat fast food (for lunch and sometimes dinner). Disappointment. Failure. Embarrassment. Check, check, check.

There are so many embarrassing moments in my life I wish I could erase, parts of me I wish I could cut off like split ends. I cover so much of me with a lovely, have-it-all-together exterior. I cover my shame with anything that won't let out my secret that

I am a sham inside. There are so many experiences from my past that make me quiver, but crying in front of my therapist over a TV show ranks near the top.

It was a few years into marriage and babies that my life and brain felt like mush. Within five years I had graduated from college and grad school, married Sam, got pregnant, and had a grumpy (but adorable) baby plus another. In that time, my family imploded, Sam's family exploded, and one of my best friends said she needed a few weeks of space from our friendship (weeks that turned into years). Sam and I were rejected from the church that practically raised us, we moved four times, and I was miserably fat from pregnancy. I couldn't seem to form cohesive thoughts without crying or getting angry at everyone. Everything inside of me hurt.

In an effort to move through the places where I felt stuck, I called a counselor and made an appointment. I had recently started watching *Friday Night Lights*. By "watching" I mean Sam and I binge-watched it on Netflix every night for hours until we could hardly keep our eyes open. It's a series about high school kids hooking up, football, and a coach becoming a father figure to lost teenagers. In my defense, the show is beautifully filmed and phenomenally written with dynamic character development, all weaved together with deep themes of trust, commitment, and redemption. It also helps that the high school boys are actually insanely attractive guys in their early thirties. Regardless, it was an addiction that took my mind off of my problems, an escape. I knew things had gone too far when about three sessions into counseling I started crying over two of the main characters in *FNL* breaking up. My counselor handled my meltdown over a fictitious high school breakup pretty well. I guess if I'm paying someone $100 an hour to listen to me rant, they need to nod their head like whatever I'm saying is the most reasonable thing they've ever heard even if they think I'm crazy! But my therapist was wise, and she listened and took in my words like they had value. Still, it was undoubtedly another embarrassing moment to add to my list. Check.

That *FNL* summer was a dark summer. I was pregnant with my third baby, Noelle, and we had moved away from family and friends. This pregnancy was more difficult than it was with my boys. There was a musty smell under the sinks and in the cupboards of our new home that made me nauseous. The thought of chicken made me feel like gagging. I was exclusively eating oranges and turkey sandwiches. I was mad all the time. It was also the summer I shot a wedding in Japan. It was one of those things I couldn't pass up, an opportunity for my photography business to expand and grow. And I was desperate for some time alone, some time away. So at 4:00 a.m. in early July, Sam helped me load my bags into the car, my cameras and lenses wrapped in T-shirts and socks, and I drove myself to the airport.

Two hours into the fifteen-hour flight, my laptop battery died. I had drained it watching *Friday Night Lights*. I ended up listening to a song by Sara Groves. Out of nowhere, when the plane was in sleep mode with only a few spotlights on like a desolate freeway at midnight, I began to cry. I cried silent tears. Crammed in the middle seat between the grandma snoring and the college student reading, with my head pressed back against the airplane seat, I wept.

I played the first line on repeat until my phone battery died too. She sang, "I was about to give up and that's no lie."[3] Sometimes our souls become so thin that any echo of beauty or melody that resonates with our fragility evokes emotion. I didn't have the words to express it, but something in me felt a release, a letting go, a moment when I could finally give up. And on this plane to a foreign country, without children or demands, I could let down and feel just how desperate I was, how ready I was to be done.

Japan was such a beautiful, mysterious, slowing-down-for-my-heart-to-see experience. Shooting the most gorgeous wedding, experiencing culture and traditions that seemed elegant and lovely and delicate absolutely humbled me. The wedding included performances and skits and a cake cutting that drew out about two hundred happy Japanese cameras, iPhones, and iPads just to capture the moment. The bride and groom read letters to their parents, and the sweet tears of a wrinkled father brought down the house. I could hardly take pictures between wiping my own tears. The day was extraordinary. From the exquisite kimonos to the bride's music selection for walking down the aisle ("Jesus Loves Me") and the game of *Jeopardy!* at the downtown reception, I was mesmerized by the wonder surrounding the day.

I took Japan in, all of it. I drank it. I felt it. I held it carefully. On the bullet train, when scenery was whizzing by, I let my eyes focus in on specific pieces of landscape, letting trees and huts and rice fields seem to freeze in my frame even though I was going over 100 miles per hour. In some ways, I felt like my life was speeding past me; I couldn't get a grip on anything, but when my eyes could lock in, everything seemed to slow down. It felt so good to see life slowly, to be present, to breathe, to exhale, to be still in a spinning world. Because of the time change, I fell asleep at 7:00 p.m. and woke up as early as 4:00 a.m. While Japan was still asleep, I'd fix my computer up onto my lap and watch the next episode of *Friday Night Lights*. When the glow of my laptop was met by the glow of the sunrise, I'd start the day.

I accepted an invitation to join the bride's family for dinner one evening. I found the restaurant at the end of an alley, and when I walked in I realized immediately I was embarrassingly under-dressed. The entire restaurant was black. Black tile flooring, black walls and curtains, black marble-topped tables with a single candle in the center. I was in a T-shirt, jeans, and flip-flops. But I was pregnant and I learned with my first pregnancy that you can pretty much get away with anything when you're pregnant—napping at all hours, eating gallons of ice cream, and wearing socks with sandals. I just hoped that the pregnant pass to do whatever you want crossed cultures. So when I got odd looks as I was escorted to our table, I just nonchalantly rubbed my belly bump and nodded my head like, "You understand, right?" And miraculously people would smile back. I thought we were connecting through our body language, but for all I knew, they were smiling, thinking, "Crazy American." Regardless, it made me feel better about my major cultural misstep.

When course after course came out, each some rendition of sushi, I started to panic. I hate fish. Knowing that my meal alone was probably in the three figures, I felt sweat beading under my armpits. So I took long, slow bites of rice, one grain at a time. I cut my portions into smaller sizes and moved my food around the plate, never actually putting a bite of fish into my mouth. I wasn't sure if rubbing my baby bump and nodding could get me out of not eating anything at that hours-long meal, but I rubbed away like a girl with a lamp, hoping for magic.

After five days traveling, shooting the wedding, and shooting the most memorable engagement session — in Tokyo, dashing through traffic, the rush of downtown and the wind blowing wildly — I was ready to go home. Ready to hug my boys and eat familiar food and see life as slowly as I did on the trains and as slowly as I ate my rice at the restaurant.

On the plane ride home, I had two different layovers and over twenty hours of traveling, so I started reading one of the books I brought. Midway through, I was hooked. Chapter after chapter, I was connecting to the author, and the words were like darts into my heart, a mixture of laughter and *aha* moments. Then the most unimaginable thing happened. Nearing page 100 the author refers to his life growing up in Texas and a movie and TV show that were based on his high school: *Friday Night Lights.* I put my book down and looked around the plane like someone was pulling a fast one on me. What in the world? The show I was crying about in counseling and watching nonstop was now the theme of the book I was reading? While flying thousands of miles over the Pacific Ocean?

I read on in amazement. The author used *Friday Night Lights* as an example of how sometimes the best stories are those of failing. I put my book down and stared out the pocket-sized window of the plane, out onto the clouds floating midair and the smear of peach and gold lavishly spread across the sky like a delicious Creamsicle. And it all clicked for me. The embarrassment I had been experiencing the past few months, and my entire life, all made sense. Shame redeemed in our lives becomes our greatest story.

I think I had been rushing and running, moving frantically throughout my days, trying to inch ahead or, more than anything, trying not to feel my shame. In my attempt to finish my days with an empty to-do list, I missed so much. It's dangerous not to accept embarrassment, even to ourselves. We cut ourselves down and put on something pretty. We push aside and push down the pain and, like the bullet train, keep moving at 100 miles per hour. There were parts of me that I hated seeing, so I set my mind on not seeing them or letting anyone else see them. My failures made me feel fractured, so I refused to look.

There are so many things about myself that I wish were different. Besides the mistakes I've made, I don't like the gap in my front teeth, my pudgy nose, my unruly eyebrows, and the pterygium (which causes redness on my eyes) that makes me look like a pothead. There are so many parts of my story that I wish I could do over again. I was so disappointed in who I had become. Disappointment is like a drug that drags me down, a weight that never lets up or lets go. I was disappointed in the things I had said, lived, and let myself love. So many moments of embarrassment, disappointment, and regret blinded me. But on that plane, between pages of a book and cumulus clouds, I realized that the parts of me I hated to see so much were the parts that God designed to use for His glory.

I needed to stop believing that God was disappointed in me the way I felt like my dad was disappointed in me. Disappointment comes attached to certain expectations. When I mess up, disappointment echoes loudly in my head. But God, He is different. And though I believe that God is grieved by our poor choices, I don't believe He is disappointed in us. Nothing surprises God. He knows us; He knows me. He is unmoved and unruffled and unsurprised when I choose selfishness over selflessness. He knows my capacity to sin and seek first *my* kingdom and *my* will above His. My failure and mistakes are never met with shock when I come to the Savior. I am never met with God's admonition, "Try better or harder or more." I am met with "Come a little closer."

Not only is God not disappointed in us, but He actually delights in us. Not only does God love us, but He likes us too. I think God delighted in the mysterious coordination of a book, a plane, my favorite TV show, and a kaleidoscope of colors in the sky—all to remind me that I am loved. I think God moves into the little cracks and crevices and corners of our lives to surprise us with His delight.

We cover ourselves with nicely coordinated outfits, a Pottery Barn family room, and well-behaved kids. We cover ourselves with perfectly angled selfies, our children's report cards, politically correct sentences, and organized shelves. I think there is something inside of me that just feels wrong or off or bad. This "I am bad" feeling is shame. That deep belief that something is wrong isn't just from nurture, but from nature. It is the same feeling that drove Eve to cover herself and hide from God in the garden. Shame is a result of my disordered desires. I desire entertainment, but too much of it. I want food, but I'm obsessed with it every waking moment. I long for intimacy, so I stay in toxic relationships trying to get it. Shame makes me panic and put on anything to cover up my "I am bad" feelings. I try so hard to convince others and myself that I'm not bad, but actually good.

Yet, my coverings are insufficient and never enough to blot out what feels so broken. All the self-esteem, pep talks, and counseling in the world can't seem to remove the wound in my soul that tells me something's desperately wrong. I know God, through Christ, makes me new. I know the cross makes things right. I know His blood covers me. But why—why do I still feel awful inside? Why am I so painfully stuck in shame and obsessed with people's approval?

I've been stuck in this place for so long. I'm trapped right here. Sometimes shame makes me feel like I'm suffocating, but it can also make me feel safe. It keeps me feeling in control. If I don't cover my bad, I have to see and feel my bad. If I'm honest, I don't want to see my heart and experience those terrifying realities. Even if it is exhausting, I'd rather keep the show going. I'd rather pretend I've got it all together than feel how lousy, lonely, and lost I am on the inside.

Perhaps this is where God moves in. Right here. He moves right into the place where my performance cracks. He interrupts my cover and shame cycle by making it nearly impossible to keep the charade going. It's when I'm caught in a little lie, people see my messy car, or I make a spelling error in an important email that I'm exposed. When I can't manage everyone's expectations, contain my child's tantrum, or remember someone's name, I'm embarrassed. My cover is blown. When I crack, break, or shut down, it makes a way for His Spirit to intervene. It becomes an "I'm coming after the real you" intervention from God.

In love, He finds me under all the ways I've tried to make myself look good. God invites me to see my shame instead of shooing it away. Shame becomes the sign on the highway leading me back to Him. When I feel shame it is like an alarm for my soul that screams, "You are trying to prove yourself again!" But God. God reminds me that I have nothing to prove. Any corruption or bad inside of me was atoned for on the cross. *This* is where I stand. *This* is where I rise. *This* is where I stay and remember who I am. I am a child of God. *This* is where I begin to believe that God loves me; way down, under it all, He loves me. Jesus turns all my bent-out, turned-in, twisted-around brokenness into this—goodness. God looks at me and repeats the words spoken after the world's completion. Through Jesus, He can look straight at my insides, smile, and say, "She is good" (see Genesis 1:31).

He delights in loving me, a girl who's made a million mistakes. It is the kind of delight that met me sky high on a plane over the Pacific. His love reminded me that my failures and cultural no-no's are actually the greatest, brightest parts of my story. The things I regret and actions I wish I could take back, the people I've hurt and names I've slandered and relationships I shattered aren't stories that are meant to live and die under heaps of shame. And though I want to fast-forward through the embarrassment of kissing boys I never should have been with, I know allowing God into all those places is the pathway to freedom. God is in a rigorous and passionate pursuit of my soul. He won't stop until He takes me to my depths, into my hidden heart. He wants to reveal to me my hollowness, my whitewashed tomb. I see how God is always at work pointing me to my wounds. He tirelessly strips back my tactics to keep people out and the truth of who I am in. He doesn't want me to live one life on the inside and a different one on the outside. He wants me to be one, whole, free.

Japan changed me. Well, God changed me. And it was through a TV show I was obsessed with. Parts of me that once made me cringe in shame are now being covered in love and are launching places to tell my story, embarrassments and all.

Shame redeemed
in our lives
becomes our
greatest story.

14

WHAT RISSA SAID

An Invitation to Scarcity

My mom is the most generous person I know. I grew up watching her pack up the food from our fridge into Ziploc bags and hand it out to strangers who walked through our doors. At restaurants when the check arrived, my mom would hand her credit card back to our server and whisper that she wanted to pay for the food ordered by the people at a nearby table. Several times when we were in line at the market, my mom swooped in and swiped her credit card first and paid for the customer in front of us. She gave furniture away without flinching, picked up hitchhikers, and bought out all the boxes of Girl Scout cookies just to encourage the little girls outside the grocery store. My mom is a car salesman's dream client. It is never about the product; it is always about the person. Her generosity wasn't because there was an abundance of money in our home growing up. My parents were missionaries. We didn't go on shopping sprees, take Disneyland vacations, or buy new clothes. We didn't have much, but what my parents had, they shared and, mysteriously, we always lived with abundance. Money's only function for my mom was as a means to love.

Generosity was modeled beautifully by my parents by the way they have opened their home to international college students for over forty-five years, filling their bellies and feeding their souls with Jesus. They didn't count their pennies and cling to their possessions or panic about their savings account. They gave and gave and gave. Even though I grew up in a home where generosity was abundant, I still felt anxious to keep a little for myself. I'm always a little afraid the funds will run out. I want to be generous and buy a meal for the guy on the corner like my mom did, but something always stops me. I calculate, count, pick and choose how generous I want to be. Generosity, for me, always feels conflicting. If I give, there won't be enough for me. I'm scared of scarcity. I always want to know there will be enough left over.

Anxiety about money burrows just below my rib cage and jabs me. Sometimes I feel like it wraps around my throat, making it hard to breathe. I am quick to judge the way others spend or don't spend it. When topics like yearly salaries or bankruptcy or debt come up in conversation, I get fidgety as if someone has food stuck in their teeth, and I can't focus on the words they are saying—just the awkwardness I feel. Money messes with me. It is the source of arguments and ceaseless worry. The worry that money brings feels like I'm walking around wearing a wet blanket, heavy and oppressive.

I can't tell you how many times Sam and I made a plan on "how to climb out of debt." I have a running Christmas wish list all year long. Just today I added new wood floors, Bobby Brown makeup brushes, a fabulous pair of high-waisted linen pants, and new sheets. My want list is endless and feels intoxicatingly urgent at times. The jittery angst that money gives me lives just below the surface of the everyday decisions I make.

I was tired of living paycheck to paycheck. Sam was a youth pastor and just finishing his seventh year of grad school. I was growing my business and popping out babies. We were paying off school loans and trying to resurrect our credit score. I just wanted to catch up, to exhale. I wanted to feel secure and to put just a little into savings. I was tired of constantly struggling. I was jealous of people who could go on vacation, buy the good cheese, or get every new iPhone that came out. Somehow I was convinced that if we could just get to a specific financial place, then everything would be okay. But we just couldn't get ahead. The car broke down or the kids required new shoes just when I felt like we were getting to a good financial place. I was frustrated as if I was hitting every red light while everyone else cruised through the green ones.

In the middle of my adult-sized tantrum, I had a conversation with my wise friend Rissa. I call her wise because she is. She really loves Jesus and really lives that way. I vented about our finances to her. She listened. Rissa told me she knew the secret to being free from money and the anxiety it provokes. I leaned in curiously. She said two words: "Give more." I wasn't expecting the solution to my financial struggle would be to actually give away my money. I was so focused on how to get more that the thought of giving more money away never entered my mind. But she is wise, so I thought I'd give it a try. She was right; it changed everything.

Before Rissa's wise words, when I thought of gifting a friend or stranger food or clothing, I would instantly shut down the idea. When I thought of inviting people over to our crammed house, offering to babysit for a friend in need, or giving more to the church, I'd rationalize away all the reasons why we shouldn't do it: we are trying to save money for a house, I couldn't get myself something else I wanted, my hands were too full, we couldn't reach our financial goals, my time is limited, etc. I am an excellent rationalizer when I need to be.

But after Rissa said those words, I stopped ticking off all my reasons not to give. When giving opportunities surfaced in my mind, I didn't automatically swat them away; I stayed with them and prayed about them. When I had the nudge to give more, I did. My fists went from clenched to open. My heart went from tight to trust. I think those nudges are straight from the Spirit. I don't always know why He impresses upon me to give, but I do know when I listen and follow through, despite my fear, I'm walking in alignment with God's will.

I've spent so much of my life nervous about how I'm going to get more. When my intentions shifted to how to give more, I started to see that generosity wasn't just about meeting the monetary needs of others. It was so much more than that. My generosity had the power to briefly lift the anxiety that presses people down. For that moment, they tangibly see God. They get a peek into eternity. They experience, ever so slightly, a taste of heaven—a place with boundless resources. Generosity lifts the veil from the earthly realm and lets people see into the heavenly realm.

Sometimes I feel like I'm standing on one side of a revolving door with eternity on the other side. Generosity puts into motion the glass passageway—giving me a flickering glimpse of the other side. It's a glorious foreshadowing of what's to come. Grace, forgiveness, mercy, compassion, and selflessness, when extended to another in generosity, blow open the walls of our world and give us a picture of the world that has yet to come. God invites us into this whimsical dance of generosity. He allows us to be partakers and peace offerers. Generosity lifts the fear and panic and impulse to store away for ourselves. Greed pressures us to use others for our gain, causes us to nervously pinch pennies, and fills us with jealous rage. It suffocates and shrinks us. But, generosity. Oh, the soul-opening gift of generosity moves us to a Narnia-like wardrobe transporting us from present time and into eternity.

Some people live as though another world is coming. This earth isn't their home. I'm thankful for my mom and Rissa. They are this kind of person. I'm thankful for my friend Ashley, a single mom who lavishly spoils me with flowers, listening, and babysitting. I'm thankful for my friend Kristin, who never comes over empty-handed but with her best baked goods, and my sisters, who generously love me by loving my kids. They help me gaze into the face of God's overwhelming comfort and goodwill toward me. They help me see heaven—a place where life is without fear or heartache, pain or scarcity. Their generosity bends back the physical layers marked by sky, stars, and streams and lets me see into the heavenly ones marked by sparkling emerald gates, lavish gold streets, and a love reunion with every soul who's ever gone before me. Generosity pries open my eyes to see what life is really all about. It's not about the here and now or the get, get, get. It's not about more, more, more. Eternity is endless grace, endless mercy, endless goodness, endless joy, and never-ending, boundless, never-running-out love. It's about eternity with Jesus. It is forever being with the Person who, in captivated delight, can't take His eyes off of me.

I'm learning to give. When fears threaten to make me stop giving, I know I'm at the brink of something good. When the groans of giving scare me into withholding, I know a gift is waiting for me right there.

So, I stay with the uneasy itch that comes with scarcity. I stay in the nervousness that comes when my account is in the single digits. I wait right there because I believe that generosity is at the center of God's heartbeat. I stay drastically close to being irresponsible because I want, with all of my being, to be close to God.

At the beginning of my emptiness is the place I actually start growing. As much as I want to be comfortable, I want to grow more—I want God more. I don't want to stay stagnant and still and the same. I want my soul stretched out like dough pressed down and pulled wide apart, the only way for it to rise well. I want to see God today. He is inviting me to see into eternity. My scarcity is a gift that moves me into my vulnerability, my fragility, and my need for greater reliance on God, who gives endlessly. I want to be as absurd as my mom, who gives away everything she owns to people who don't deserve it. She lives her life like there is another one around the bend.

When my parents were young, poor, and eating ramen noodles for every meal, they only had one dollar to their name. One. It wasn't enough for diapers, milk, or tuna fish for the family. They had one dollar and two young daughters. At Sunday night church the preacher taught on the widow's mite—a story about a woman who gave everything she had to God, which was approximately three dollars. My mom looked at my dad, and their eye contact spoke in united agreement. My dad dipped his hand into his pocket and pulled out their one remaining dollar. As the offering basket passed by, he put their final dollar and all of his faith into that bowl. Moments later a man tapped him on the shoulder and handed him a ten-dollar bill. They were overwhelmed with tears of awe and amazement at the generosity of a man they barely knew.

My mom retold this story at a women's event weeks later. She spoke about putting all your trust in Jesus. After the event, a woman named Bonnie came up to her and asked if she needed milk. My mom nodded. For the next nineteen and a half years, Bonnie and her husband paid for milk to be delivered to their doorstep. Every Friday and every Monday, milkmen would pull up to our farmhouse in a white van and carry the milk cartons right into our refrigerator. A gallon and a half on Friday and two gallons on

Monday. There was never a shortage of milk. The very last gallon was delivered days after I moved out and away to college. God gave my parents provision over their family in the most unexpected way. Give, give, give. There is always a heaven-sized miracle waiting to happen.

Eternity is endless grace, endless mercy, endless goodness, endless joy, and never-ending, boundless, never-running-out love.

15

NOELLE HOPE

An Invitation to Wait

hanksgiving is my favorite holiday because of the mere fact that it revolves around food, lots of it. I was thirty-six-weeks pregnant with my third baby, but my first girl, when thirty of us sat around an enormous dinner table jammed with kids, warm bodies, and shoulders overlapping shoulders, shoveling down deep-fried turkey and my favorite mushy, flavor-filled green beans. My sister played the piano as she does after every holiday dinner. We gathered the remnants of a meal much enjoyed: dishes, plates, platters, and bowls literally licked clean.

My brother-in-law conveniently always has to go to the bathroom right when the cleaning starts, and thirty minutes later, he reappears when dessert is being served. We laughed and rolled our eyes as he grabbed a magazine and headed for the bathroom, singing,

"Make me a servant, humble and meek." I joined the assembly line, and one sister handed me plates. I rinsed and passed them to another sister to dry, my belly ripe with baby. As I rinsed, belly button rubbing the edge of the sink, I noted the moment, savored it. The music, the joy, the noise, the people I loved moving in and out of rooms, my baby kicking. There was so much anticipation. The thrill and the excitement of Christmas only weeks away; tiny toes and little eyes cracking open to see color for the first time felt so close. Moments like these feel as though life is falling the way I dreamed it would. And things like music and a missing brother-in-law become the good stories we tell.

The day after that Thanksgiving, in the darkness of night, I went into early labor. Despite the disbelief (and minor dispute with Sam), we went to the hospital, and I gave birth to Noelle Hope, 5 pounds and 5 ounces. I barely caught a glimpse of her fuzzy blond hair, her father's lips, and my dimpled chin before nurses whisked her away. Her vitals were unstable. I waited as they finished sewing up my wound, a scar that bears the names of all my babies. I waited in the recovery room, silent and alone. Sam met me and whispered all of Noelle's beauties into my ear: her delicate hands and fresh baby smell. He told me gently we had to wait to hold her because her heart rate was irregular.

We had to wait.

My body numb from medication, my heart tightened in the tension of the unknown.

I waited and begged nurses to see Noelle. I waited and waited some more. How many times have I lived in the dreadful tension of waiting: waiting for a doctor to call with results, for pain to pass, for money to appear, for heaven to come, for someone to love me back or the way they should? I spent years waiting for things to change, for friends to come around, for parents to approve, for someone to come back home, back to Jesus. I've wept and waited and pleaded with God to intervene. I hear it in my shaky voice, "O God, O God, I beg you. Come, please come. Please change, move, release, heal."

In the waiting, I feel the tension. I push up against my fragile anxiety in all the in-between moments. I push up against the dissatisfaction that life wasn't supposed to be the way it is. Marriages aren't meant to fail, crack, and fall apart. Mothers aren't meant to spiral into depression. Careers are supposed to flourish, relationships bloom, and hearts remain soft, kind, and open. Sisters support each other, parents live forever, and friends stay loyal. This year, the reality snuck up on me again; life is far from easy. The panic in my friend's voice describing her estranged husband showing up drunk, again, reminded me. Doctors confirming a brain tumor in my friend's two-year-old son reminded me. The reminder came when I answered the phone to the tears of a friend whose husband had fallen hard back into sexual addiction and when I received a text reading, "Pray, I'm bleeding. Miscarriage. Again." When the monstrous, evil, dark cloud of death seems to visit the same households again and again, I am reminded that pain is so deep and so wide it threatens to swallow me whole. The pain closes in on me like my shadow in the midday sun. So much of life is silently mourning the way life is and mourning the way life isn't.

I can't will my life circumstances to change; I can't force or make people do things; I can't fix my situation. In the waiting, I feel powerless, out of control. I scrape at anything for understanding. I pace in the "what-ifs" and "how comes." I can't do enough research to release me from the grip that tension has on me in the waiting. In the tension I see what I desperately want. The waiting draws out my true longings. I see what I crave, cling to, and hope for.

I see myself raw and real in the waiting.

I'm tempted to believe that God is unloving or that He intends to withhold good from me to teach me some sort of life lesson. God feels distant and untrustworthy, cruel and apathetic, disinterested and unplugged from my pain. I cringe at simple answers and catchy Christian comebacks. I can't reconcile a good God with the evil in the world. I can't. I can't make sense of God's sovereignty in a world of suffering. I can only do one thing.

I can be in the waiting. I can express, again and again, the agony and unfairness of feeling forgotten. I can explode like a busted pipe, without control or aim, water jetting out all over the place. I can bleed my pain. I can feel it sticky, pointed, and sharp with sensitivity like a cactus to a single touch. I can scream in outrage at all that is unjustly broken. My heart sickness can find comfort with blinds shut, doors locked, and covers pulled down tight across my chest. I can fall on the floor and sob with my body hard pressed to the ground, my sorrow huge and suffocating. I can be silent and stiff and frozen solid in sadness that life isn't as I hoped it would be. I can invite others to wait with me. In the waiting there is boredom, disbelief, and apathy. These are feelings too. The invitation isn't to think my feelings, but to feel them. I have to feel them: rattling, relentless, and inescapable. I have to weep, complain, shake, and hurt until I can hardly keep my head up. The only possible way to endure the long season of waiting is to settle into it with all of my being, might, will, and fortitude. I have to stay in it. God doesn't always answer my questions, but He insists on sitting with me in them. The invitation is to lament.

I'm learning not to rush the waiting. Don't hurry the kids to grow up, don't skip over the grief, don't run from sticky relationships. I try not to shut off my desires, pretend I don't care, flounder in self-pity, or force open doors. In the angst or anticipation, I am learning to hold on to those in-between moments. In the waiting room, even there, good can be found. The waiting room is an incubator of sorts, a place for me to stay warm, held, and protected in my pain. A place I can be weak, soul sick, and undone. God is swaddling me up in a cloak of love. He is delicately sewing my soul into perfect relationship with Him, stitch by stitch, slowly and precisely. I'm learning patience. I have to trust that one day I'll look back and see just how lovely I became through the long, excruciating seasons of "hold on and wait."

With this hope I can sing with tears effortlessly flowing down my face, "Till He appeared, and the soul felt its worth."[4] My very soul is given substance. I matter. No matter what the waiting is, no matter what the pain is, no matter how long I've cried out in anguish, I will endure. I will carry on. I won't give up, I won't shut out, shut down, or shut in. I will stay in the shadow of death because in the wandering tension of waiting, I don't wait alone.

I waited all night to hold my baby girl. Darkness, a cold companion to my fears, was being met by morning light. Then, there she was. My Noelle. My hope. My Christmas gift come early. I felt unworthy to hold such a tender soul. Bare skin against bare skin, they laid her on my chest, her limp head against my heart. Hot tears released. I breathed in. I breathed out. My shaking hand against the whole of her wrinkled back, I breathed. I whispered, "*Breathe. Slow your heart to mine.*" She lay, sweetly panting, desperately trying to catch her breath. It is the same whisper of God to me in all my waiting: "*Slow your heart to mine.*"

We breathed together, my baby girl and I. Bodies rising and falling at ease. Her heart rate falling in sync with mine. After I held Noelle, she didn't require any more assistance, but found healing right on my bosom. We breathed together, healthy, whole, as one.

EXPOSED

An Invitation to Come Out of Hiding

I knew I should be happy, but I was completely unraveling. Days earlier I received a phone call from my dear friend's mom, Martha. Martha has always been one of those moms I felt I could sit down and flip through a Gap catalog with or share my latest relationship drama with. She was intentional about inviting me to dinner and commenting on my blog posts, but her call one fall morning was completely unexpected. She offered to help me one day a week so I could have a break. I was shocked. I was grinning and taken aback and surprised that she would give up her freedom, come to my home, and hold my baby while I went out and did whatever I wanted to. I mean *whatever* I wanted to do. For a momma with three little kids, the freedom to roam the aisles of Target indefinitely or actually try clothes on in a dressing room instead of ripping them off hangers like a madwoman on a timed shopping spree or eat a meal as slowly as I wanted—I was itching for this kind of freedom. Martha was giving me a reason to wear mascara again.

When I hung up the phone, I instantly got knots in my stomach. I couldn't sleep that night or the next. I was angry that I wasn't happy and bothered that I couldn't just say yes to her generous offer. Here was my opportunity for a few minutes of alone in my baby-hazed, frumpy, toddler-tantruming, endless momma days. But something in me hesitated. I wanted to say, "Yes, when can we start?" but after two days passed, I told her, "No, thank you."

I love my children but struggled desperately with day-to-day motherhood duties. My oldest was as strong-willed as a bulldog, always in attack stance. More often than not, this five-year-old and I ended up in a yelling match. Sitting him in front of the TV was the quickest way to quiet I could find, so he sat there for hours.

When my second son, Samuel, was a year old, he only weighed sixteen pounds. This officially put him in the FTT category. FTT stands for "failure to thrive." It is a nice little abbreviation, but interpreted by a tired mom it means "Hey, you suck." Samuel couldn't gain weight. We did tons of tests, practically poured calories down his throat, and visited several specialists. I remember sitting in the waiting room while Sam held him and the nurse drew buckets of his blood. My baby's screams echoed so loudly the entire waiting room felt a chill. And I sat, head bowed, eyes tight, with tears slipping silently down my face, listening to the horror of my little boy in pain.

Feeding Samuel was a chore. It took a tremendous amount of effort to get food in his mouth and down his throat. In order for him to eat, I had to feed him, bite by bite. I had to bribe him, distract him with TV, and sneak in food any way I could. I dreaded mealtime. Somehow breakfast, lunch, and dinner felt like they were constantly pounding on my door. He was three when Martha offered to help. I was still forcing him to sit beside me while I jammed food into his mouth in between pausing shows on the iPad.

Noelle was my darling little girl who spent hours of her babyhood strapped into a car seat while I ran errands and boys to soccer practice. When she wasn't in the car, I was nursing her, napping her, or fastening her into a swing. I didn't know how to entertain her and wrangle my world of rising responsibilities.

I didn't show people this side of my life. I would let people see my latest photographed wedding being featured or published, but I didn't let people see my little secrets. People didn't know how much TV Manoah actually watched and how I force-fed Samuel or let the equipment soothe Noelle. I felt like I was failing at everything. My boys were like wrecking balls. They were noisy, messy, and naked most of the time. All these parts of my parenting drove me into hiding. The thought of someone seeing my secrets scared me. If anyone knew how I coped through the day with screens, candy, and bribing I would be mortified. That's why I said no to Martha even though my heart begged for a reason to curl my hair in the morning and window-shop at the mall with a coffee in hand like I was twenty.

I couldn't let anyone see the truth. It would be terrifying. It's like that mortifying moment when I see yellow gunk oozing out of one of my kids' ears or dirt crusted under their freakishly long fingernails—sure signs I am failing at motherhood. Little signals that I'm not a fit parent. When these show up in my kids, I pray to God that their teacher, the cashier at the grocery store, or my morning playdate mom didn't see them first.

I am exposed every time I take my kids to the doctor. When I check them in and the receptionist asks if I have their immunization card, I fumble through my purse for a minute pretending it's in there—an act. Then I say I must have left it on the kitchen table or the car. But if I was really being honest, I would say I haven't seen that yellow piece of paper since my kid was born. It is probably stuffed into a box in our garage somewhere between the Christmas ornaments and my grad school papers. (While I'm on the subject, in the twenty-first century, when the entire world has transferred from paper to digital, why in the world are we—delirious and sleep-deprived mothers—still responsible for this information, only kept on a flimsy piece of card stock? Are our children's important immunization records really safe in a Ziploc bag in the hands of a tired momma who regularly finds herself putting milk away in the pantry? In the age of healthcare reformation, please, can we do something about these immunization cards?) I leave every doctor's appointment guilty about something. I nod with a confident, "Absolutely," when the pediatrician asks if the kids are getting all their fruits and vegetables, and if I'm reading to them for at least thirty minutes a day.

I can't stand the idea of people seeing my secret failures. My weaknesses are perfectly kept behind closed doors, off of social media, out of conversation, and in that box with the immunization cards. I'm a professional at keeping the disgraceful parts of my parenting behind closed doors and just for me, thank you very much.

After turning Martha's offer down, I wrestled with my decision. I called her back and invited her for tea. The boys were away and Noelle napped while we sat with my farmhouse table between us and bared our souls over sips of Earl Grey. I told her the real reason I declined her gracious offer. I told her about how Manoah doesn't listen to me. I can't get Samuel to eat. I told her that I feel guilty about everything. I went on and on. I went on about my laundry, and how there are baskets filled with clean laundry that somehow get mixed up with dirty clothes. I can't tell them apart, so I just end up dumping all the clothes, clean and dirty, back into the washing machine. I told her about my floors covered in cereal and Legos and my pantry that looked like it was hit by a hurricane and how I didn't have any part of my life together. I went down my long list, certain I'd scare her away, but the more I shared, the more a smile spread across her face, like nothing I said seemed to surprise her.

In the most unexpected moment, in the moment when Martha should have kindly withdrawn her offer, she asked if she could start on Thursday. She told me to leave the laundry out and just show her where I kept my broom. She gave me some of the best parenting advice I've ever gotten. She told me she had been there, that all moms have, but no one wants to talk about it. Essentially, she told me I wasn't alone; everyone has their secrets. I was convinced that no one else was as terrible as I was. Were other moms missing important papers and deadlines? Was it possible other moms didn't scrub their bathroom floors or that their car seats were growing mold? I'm not sure, but I am certain of one thing: all moms experience guilt.

I know this may sound strange, but guilt isn't a feeling. I can't feel guilt. So often we confuse guilt and shame, but they are not the same. Guilt is right and wrong, black and white. You can be guilty whether you feel it or not. Guilt is *I've done bad*. Shame is *I feel bad*. When I am guilty, what I feel is fear. It is the fear of being found out, discovered, or exposed for what I've done. Fear drives me into hiding, into pretending, into the shadows. The monster of mom-guilt is real. It's loud and terrifying and scary. There have been so many voices whispering and screaming at me since the moment I became a mom. I hear so many *shoulds* and *musts*. Some are from church, culture, my mother-in-law, or social media. But most of them rise up from inside of me. The fear of being found out for being a mom who makes a ton of mistakes terrifies me. I'm afraid I'm letting my kids down. I'm afraid I'm not doing enough. I'm afraid people will think I'm a bad mom or, worse, that I actually am a bad mom. I'm just so afraid. All the time.

I hide my guilt behind accomplishments and, even worse, my kids' accomplishments. I wear my kids as accessories. I hide my guilt with adventures and activities. I hide the insecurities of motherhood by talking about how well my kids sleep or clean up or color. Guilt came from the garden. Guilt drove Eve into hiding. Her fear is my fear, and I silence my guilt by disappearing into the darkness. Worry pounds so loudly in the heart of a mother. It screams at me in my stress. It repeatedly mocks my attempts to care for little souls. As I sit on the floor of the bathroom during work hours pumping breast milk, the hum of sound waves in and out murmur, "You are a failure. You are a failure. You are a failure." I do all I can to outrun the guilt. I hide and pretend it isn't there. But it echoes all the louder and all the more.

I shared with Martha that I felt beat up from mothering. Dizzy, exhausted, and spent. Instantly, hot tears burned down my cheeks. I was doing all that I could just to survive. Everything felt empty. My accomplishments that day: shushing a baby to sleep, making little lunches that went uneaten, vacuuming smashed goldfish crackers out of our rug—twice—finding the remote control drowning in water, trying to salvage a sippy cup with three-week-old curdled milk from the trunk of the car; all of these things added up to one thing—nothing. I couldn't keep up, and my guilt was piling up. I was floundering under dishes and "don't touch that" and rebuilding blanket forts. I hadn't read to them before bed in weeks, bathed them in days, or flossed their teeth—ever. My salty tears were really saying, "I'm not enough for them." I was so undone. The fear, the guilt, the massive amount of pressure broke me.

My identity was dying, and dying is painful. I was out of control like a toddler coming down off of a sugar high. Guilt was strangling me to death. But guilt can't be controlled. It can't be wrestled, smothered, or negotiated away. Guilt must be named and fear must be followed if freedom is ever to be found.

There must be kindness and discernment and patience when I explore the real source of my fear. I'm far from being the mom I want to be, but when it comes to mom-guilt, I need to shift my heart and evaluate whether my guilt is true guilt or false guilt. Have I actually done anything wrong (sinful)? There is a profound difference between false guilt and true guilt. The texture of false guilt will always push me to do more and try harder. It will keep me pretending and hiding in the fear of being found out. It will pester me with lies. It is induced by my need for human approval and personal perfection. It will heighten my anxiety and bolster my neurotic need to keep the truth sealed shut. But true guilt is so different. True guilt will always lead me back to the cross, back to my need for Christ. Real guilt will keep me humble, calm, and connected to Jesus. It will keep me vulnerable and soft.

I was guilty. But I was really only guilty of one thing—not receiving God's love for me. I needed rescuing and thought the rope to pull me up would be my parenting. I needed, more than anything, to know my value wasn't found in how good a mom I was. I needed to know, in my heart, that I mattered: me, just plain ol' messy, unkempt, complex, confused, sloppy, and drive-thru-again-for-dinner me. I mattered.

I mattered enough for God to call me out of guilt, fear, and darkness. Guilt doesn't shrink in the dark, it grows. My mom-guilt monster gets louder and scarier when it's hidden. The path isn't to shut down, silence, run away from, or bully my fear, but to follow it. I attend to it, stay awake to it, listen to it. I follow my fear to see what I am actually guilty of. I can get so caught up in dismantling my fear that I miss where it intends to take me. Anxiety, as my seminary professor always said, "is the warning light on the dashboard of my soul." Anxiety is the lighthouse in the storm leading me back to my tender need for God. It is a flare signaling me back to forgiveness, where any wrong I have done is made right. In other words, fear becomes a gift because it always leads me back to God's love.

If I am truly guilty, I deal with it with my friend Jesus. I vent and complain and confess myself all the way to Him. In the good, hard, and beautiful, I whisper to Jesus. I set my heart in a posture of prayer. A posture of daily, hourly, moment-by-moment need of His love. I am desperate for His love and to know my identity is secure in Him.

The secret of who I am is wrapped and nestled deeply in who God calls me to be. My freedom from guilt is written on the storyboard of history and spelled out on the ceiling of clouds curbing earth from outer space, keeping all of life contained. A story written across oceans, calming souls. It is written in His Word and in our hearts.

He is the God that pursues the heart of the woman in hiding. He is the God who came and covered the world — in, out, and through love. He is the God who had compassion on a grieving maidservant, blessing her with an abundance of children: Hagar. He is the God who opened the womb of a woman who had given up on her deepest dreams: Sarah. He is the God whose heart came close to a forgotten sister, one with unattractive features and an insecure heart: Leah. He is the God who found value in the socially devalued and sexually impure outcast in her community: Rahab. He is the God who bent low to bring life back to the embittered heart of a woman who had lost her husband and sons to death: Naomi. He is the God who heard the begging and pleading and heartsick, sobbing prayers of a woman longing for a child: Hannah. He is the God who heals the sick: the bleeding woman. He is the God who gives living water to the unworthy with many shameful secrets: the woman at the well. He is the God who came to the sinful and had mercy when others wanted her murdered: the adulterous woman.

He is the God who found a woman who pretended to have it all together. A woman who got pregnant when so many said she couldn't. A woman who struggles with sacrificing her career, time, slim thighs, and sleeping in for her babies. A woman who squeezes little arms far too tightly when taking them into a time-out. A woman impatient and empty. A woman jealous and constantly comparing herself to others. A woman who looks for the failures in others to feel better about herself. A girl in a fog most days, forgetting her purpose and value and meaning in everyday moments. A girl desperate for significance, praise, and influence. He is the God who makes a way for the average, the angry, and the addicted to approval: me.

I'm trying to speak honestly about my struggles as a mom. I'm done with the secrets. They only haunt and bury me. There is (and will always be) only one thing in the entire world I am guilty of—not receiving the love of God. That's it. False guilt will always try to squirm its way into my life. It will rattle me and spin me, but after I wrestle and try to fix myself for the thousandth time, I come back to truth—or maybe truth comes back to me. I rest on the reality that God rescued me out of hiding through the forgiveness of my sin on the cross. Every moment since then, the invitation to come out of hiding comes to me. Sometimes it's abrupt and loud; other times it is almost silent. But the invitation is always the same: "I see you in the darkness, come out into the light." Jesus calls me out of hiding like He called Lazarus out of death: "Come out!" (John 11:43). Come out of the darkness, come out of the grave, come a little closer and let me love you.

The words that sealed Christ's death now call me out of my shadows: "It is finished" (John 19:30). My slate is wiped clean. My soul is as smooth as marble. It is as white as a wedding gown, blindingly beautiful. When false guilt yanks incessantly on my soul, I say the words, "It is finished." When I feel afraid because everyone else is doing motherhood with more finesse, I put my fist on the table and speak, "It is finished." When evil taunts me with my mistakes, past failures, or inadequacies, I cling to those three words. When false guilt mocks me because I work, I should do more, or I should discipline differently, I say with authority, "It. Is. Finished." Those accusations are not true. I could let false guilt torture me, but I'm standing up to it. My need to get or gain approval has already been accounted for. False guilt has no place here. It can no longer tell me who I am, press me under, or turn me upside down. When truth is spoken, false guilt loses its power. I find forgiveness for what I've actually done wrong. I am pure. I am wanted. I am loved.

From the fall (when Southern California women wear boots and scarves in San Diego's 75-degree weather) to the hazy early June summer days, Martha came knocking on my door every Thursday morning. She was never empty-handed but came bearing her latest Pinterest experiment: banana nut bread with cinnamon swirl crust, chocolate brownies infused with caramel, and, my favorite, homemade roasted-strawberry balsamic ice cream. She would come; I would go. I would leave her baskets of unfolded laundry, dishes in the sink, and floors coated in muddy footprints. When I returned, the clothes were put away, my baby was napping, and the floors were immaculate. One Thursday Martha reorganized my pantry and kindly reported that I didn't need to buy any more baking powder because I had four cans of it stashed between the peanut butter and flour. Martha delighted in loving me, pouring her blessings into all my weaknesses, and caring for all the places I was too guilty to show. Thursday mornings became a discipline in coming out of hiding, recollecting who I was, and the slow shrinking of my guilt as I let love in the door.

Guilt must be named and fear must be followed if freedom is ever to be found.

17

OLD SPAGHETTI FACTORY

An Invitation to Hold On

In eighth grade, when none of my friends could drive, we packed into our parents' minivans and the moms drove us south to downtown San Diego. That first Christmas, a dozen girls celebrated the holidays together the only way we knew how, with spaghetti, Shirley Temples, and free garlic bread. Our Christmas tradition evolved a bit, but every year we carpooled down to the Old Spaghetti Factory. Now, in our thirties, we are the parents, and we drive our own minivans. The group has dwindled down to five: all married, all moms, all friends since we were in the single digits. As the holidays approach, the texting and schedules circulate as we plug our Christmas dinner into our calendars.

I like to use the metaphor of rooms in a house to describe friendships. Some friends are dining room friends. You can talk about formal and polite topics with them. Some friends are kitchen friends. You can drink wine together and cut onions and share recipes. While other friends are master bedroom friends. These are the friends that see your messy closets, your unmade bed, your unkempt floors. Friends can move from room to room too. I've had friends who were master bedroom friends leave and move to the front porch. That sucks. It's painful. That kind of rejection can take years to recover from. My Old Spaghetti Factory friends are my master bedroom people: Krissa, Mindy, Becca, and Kara. I've let them all the way in. These are the friends I can share deodorant with, borrow clothes from, and pee in front of with the door open.

These friends are the ones I've lived life with since I was still losing teeth. Our friendships evolved around school and youth group and endless summers at the beach. We all fought and back-stabbed one another at some point; we stole boyfriends and gossiped endlessly. We set each other up on blind dates and covered for each other when parents questioned whereabouts. We made dance videos, sold candy bars, performed in talent shows, and cried outside of our third-grade teacher's classroom. I don't think we ever understood that all these moments were braiding into us the cords that would bind us for a lifetime.

As we grew, sometimes we grew away from each other, but we always made an effort to meet up for our annual Christmas dinner. Somehow we always found our way back to each other: a fight with our parents that sent us to each other's doorstep, or studying for the next project, or toilet-papering at midnight. Even when we slipped down darker paths, we always knew where to find the friends who would drive us home when we had too much to drink, or tell us we were being stupid, or give us a place to spend the night when our homes were too painful to return to. Our friendships were being churned much deeper, like cream turning into butter; we were becoming soul friends. Our giggling conversations over boyfriends and shopping matured into prayer requests and callings. When questions of who to marry and which relationships to end came up, we sat together, cried together, encouraged each other, and prayed for each other.

When each one of us got engaged we threw a party and brought champagne and gushed over the ring and engagement story. We've stood by each other during vows, danced, and given toasts. And just when we thought we were done throwing parties, the babies came. Oh, the sweet, beautiful babies. With the babies came showers in pinks and blues. We made announcements and took turns hosting and planning the menus. Then after the due date had passed, we would get the call and meet at the hospital, completely enthralled and enamored with the little and newest most delicate baby, tiny toes and nose and all. And they came, one after another. The parties and prayers and strollers all meant something. Something more than writing thank-you cards and sharing baby clothes. It meant bonding and building into each other; it meant supporting and creating a structure that would hold us when the throes of life would threaten to break our bones. Because the next season in our lives would be the hardest, darkest, and most devastating; it brought out in each of us a fierceness we didn't know we had.

Friends are fierce. They battle. They defend. They show up when no one else does. This latest season in the lives of my friends has been, by far, the most brutal of them all. In the exhaustion of motherhood and babies and meltdowns, we've encountered the tragedy of broken promises, families falling apart, and children desperately ill. We've had to show up when it wasn't easy or convenient. Shattered marriages and brain tumors and short sales are never planned, not like dinner parties or birthday brunches. When one of us was unraveling, our commitment asked us to love fiercely, like never before. And so we did; we fought for each other. It wasn't always perfect, but we fought the best way we knew how, with love.

When alcoholism, addiction, and apathy crept in, when toddlers were hospitalized and battling for their lives, we prayed and paced in that dreadful waiting room. When anxiety riddled every hour, we encouraged and walked the labyrinth of worry together. When dear ones slipped, one after the next, into eternity, we supported. When the San Diego fires raged war against our city we housed or brought over extra sheets. When homes were lost, drifted away in the afternoon breeze, we helped pack boxes and unpack hearts. When filing for divorce was the only option, we waited for a miracle. When devastation tempted us to disconnect and unplug from the pain, we took turns calling and texting and showing up to fold baskets of laundry well into the night. When fathers were unfaithful and babies died on the ultrasound table, we sobbed. When one of us was afraid to attend an AA meeting alone, the other one went along. When one of us slept alone, we made a meal or brought flowers or Starbucks. When one walked through the scary doors of the counseling center, we were there to babysit and debrief. When the loneliness and wreckage of sadness threatened to overwhelm, we gathered to pray.

In this season of heartache and heaviness, our friendships became as fierce as the warrior who runs into battle instead of cowering away. And when one friend had nothing left, when giving up seemed like the only option, we lifted her tired and worn body upon the cot draped with cloth like the friends in Mark 2. We each carefully held a corner of the gurney and took her to the house where the Savior stayed. From the dirt-smothered roof, we removed the rubble, ripping away the shingles, brick by brick, prying into where hope lived. Fingernails clawing at the clay, we had to get her to Him. We knew if we could just get her dying heart before the Lord, He would heal. And when the light broke through the hole in the ceiling, we lowered her down to where Jesus waited. When all hope seemed lost, we laid down our friend before the One who brings life up from the dead. Friendship is about being the hands and feet that take the ones we love all the way to God. It is about staying even when it would be easier to leave. Love and friendship are nothing if they aren't fierce.

Our annual Christmas dinner is just around the corner. It is amazing to think we have been gathering together for so many years. In December we will all meet at the Old Spaghetti Factory. We will laugh and eat loaves of free bread. Instead of Shirley Temples, we will drink wine. Instead of pasta, we will substitute broccoli. We will be the last ones at the restaurant, until the last lick of spumoni has been slurped. We will be asked to wrap things up by the waiter. The night will end with a big group hug in the parking lot, laughing like girls, arms draped over each other, getting waves of one another's wonderful aromas. This hold is so much deeper and tighter than when we were girls playing ring-around-the-rosie. There, in that place, there is love. We are master bedroom friends. Through every season we've stayed right beside one another. We've held on even when it might have been easier to let go. When pain threatened to destroy us, we grabbed on tighter. We need each other. We need people who'll advocate for us and take us all the way to Jesus. People who will stay when there is nothing to gain, when there is no logical reason, and when it costs us everything. People who will love us with an I'm-fighting-for-you-till-the-end—no matter what—kind of love.

SAVOR

An Invitation to Grow Old

I turn forty in a few months. I type that shaking my head, with eyes wide. Wow. How did that happen? Every birthday after I turned twenty-five has come with a slice of cake and a side of anxiety. Nothing stops aging. No amount of Botox, eye cream, or dieting stops the inevitable process.

My arm skin is wiggly, my eyebrows wonky, and my face is starting to sag. My teeth are moving, and I reach for the railing when I go down stairs. Aging is weird, and no one really talks about it. People talk about how to stop aging or how to reverse the process. I live with a constant state of low-grade anxiety about growing older, buy the magical face cream at Target, and secretly dread July 14th.

Happiness is something I've always been afraid of. True, deep-down, all-out excitement actually scares me. Letting my heart fully experience the moment is something I resist. I'm reluctant to enjoy the moment because I know I can't keep it. It's so fleeting. It's why I don't get massages. Every time I'm on the table, all I can do is nervously think about how fast the time is going and so I have to enjoy, enjoy, enjoy it. The pressure to soak it in takes away the pleasure. Especially as a mom, there is an added burden to savor every single second because grandmas in the checkout line always tell me, "It goes by so fast" (as my kids are climbing the magazine rack and licking the floor). Life is moving like a bullet train. I can't do anything to slow it down. I can't stop the momentum or dig my heels into the dirt deep enough to make it all stop. The inevitable is coming. I'm afraid of death. I'm afraid of pain. I'm afraid of dying alone, in panic, gasping for air. I'm afraid of leaving my loved ones behind and the unknowns of the afterlife. I'm scared of squandering my life. These are big, gaping black holes I don't know how to deal with.

I know, in my head, that the bad, scary thing of dying has already been made good because of what God did to death. He took out the sting, trading all of our bad for His good so we wouldn't have to be alone. In pain, we aren't alone. In fear, we won't be abandoned. When our bodies turn against us, we will never be without a deep, abiding comfort. His presence is now suctioned to ours; DNA—infused to our marrow—merged, His Spirit integrated into ours. We are always spiritually alive. We are, as Lisa-Jo Baker beautifully coined, "Eternity with skin on."[5]

The worst possible part of our lives is over if we believe in Jesus. Our dead has been made alive, the curse reversed, the hole now filled. The bad thing has already happened, not just to me, but to all who believe. I know this. And to a degree it does bring me comfort. But I'm mostly still anxious when I anticipate the far-off future. I'm nervous about aging. I backpedal when I look in the mirror too long.

It's an anxiety that makes me want to avoid anything aging related. But I let the tension fill my lungs. I stay with my fears without tucking them under my to-do list or behind busyness. I whisper prayers to Jesus. I think He understands how the fear of death and the coming glory all clash and collide together. He was in the garden bleeding tears of blood, bent over, and broken—that's how much He understands. I have to look backward when I want to see forward. I have to believe that the God who walked in Eden, to the cross, with me in my most desperate time of need will, in fact, walk with me when I take my last breath. Death is scary. Terrifying, really. I don't know how I will die; I just know that I will. I have to live in the vulnerable trust that God will continue to carry me into eternity the way He has carried me since birth. Fear might tag along with me all the way till the end, but I don't want it to stop me from being alive. I want to savor life without the constant fear of it slipping away. The only way I can combat my anxiety is with gratitude. It's the pathway from knowing God is with me to experiencing peace in my soul that He actually *is* with me. It's the only way. So, I breathe in deep, breathe out slow, heart open, and give thanks.

I give thanks for the sweet smell of my afternoon tea. I relish the spicy infused flavors, warmth, and jump start it gives my body to keep going. I weep in wonder when I hold a newborn in the church nursery and give thanks for new life. I thank God for the twinkle lights like touchable stars above our backyard table. Elbows knocking, children chattering, the salty taste of corn fresh from the grill, and devoured watermelon leaving behind life-sized smiles all burst my heart open in praise. I savor. I give thanks. I applaud the Maker of the universe for making moments just like these. Thank you. Thank you. Thank you.

These sacred moments aren't just for me. Maybe God is the most excited one in the hospital room when an infant tastes life for the first time. He is there rolling up His sleeves, jumping up and down, spinning around with joy at His next and newest creation. He doesn't create a new day out of a matter-of-fact, clockmaker design, but as G. K. Chesterson says, He causes the sun to rise as "a theatrical encore."[6] God turns and tilts the world at a particular angle because He loves to watch the sun break light onto fresh earth. He eagerly anticipates the sun bursting out from behind mountains like the proud parent at the finish line waiting for their child to turn the last corner of a race: "Here it comes! Here it comes! Wait for it. . . . There it is!!!" He is thrilled with His creation. He is churning with joy over creating life over and over and over again. He claps His hands like a child at the sunrise, day after day chanting, "One more time! Let's do it again." God never tires of what we consider monotony. He delights in the joy of doing it again and again and again, not just for himself, but for us to enjoy with Him.

I'm learning to savor what God has created for me to enjoy with Him. With timidity, I'm learning to live well and full and alive, swimming from the shallow to the deep. I'm learning to float instead of frantically tread water, to sail instead of row. Even though I'm almost forty, I am discovering who I am—the things that make my heart tick and beat rapidly and rest. I don't want fear to hold me back any longer. I don't want time passing to make me panic. I want it to beckon me to live. I want to experience time like my grandpa, who collected and lined his walls with cuckoo clocks. Every hour on the hour chimes exploded throughout his home, sending a symphony of joy bouncing off the bamboo walls, a party celebrating the big hand circling back home again. I don't want to be anxious about time passing too quickly or about the squirrelly gray hair sprouting at my widow's peak. I want to age like my aunt Carol, who has sprayed the same perfume, Estée Lauder's Spellbound, across her skin for nearly thirty years. She grows in wisdom as her scent deepens in warmth.

Every day, if I pay attention, I see God inviting me into the next beautiful moment. Every day, God is nudging my heart to stay awake and savor this one incredible life. There are love winks from the Lord everywhere. He nudges the wind to move the slender branches of the olive trees lining the long hill up to my church, leaves like pom-poms cheering on my arrival. He winks at me when neighbors smile, children giggle, and food sizzles. When the massive moon feels like it's following little ol' me, and the stars make shapes I've never seen, I know God is loving me through the backdrop of blackness. If I stay awake to the world around me, I can see God's "I've got you" winks of love on an endless loop, reminding me with playfulness that the best is yet to come.

I don't want my fear to be a deterrent from all that this moment holds. So I'm going to bake cookies even when I have a tendency to burn them and buy pretty paper and write long letters to faraway friends. I'm going to rearrange my picture frames and create spaces in our house that make me sit back and smile. I'm going to wrap myself in blankets with bundles of wood popping in the fireplace and watch movies I've watched a million times. I will experience life through movement and soul-gasping beauty and sounds that make me actually feel something. I'm going to enjoy creation, believing that God is enthusiastically making the world go around and around for the mere delight of directing His own cinema for people to watch with awe, excitement, and wonder. I'm going to buy bouquets of flowers and arrange them in mason jars all over my home, even though they will die the next day. I'm going to make eye contact with myself in the mirror and give thanks for another day at life. I'm going to hold my children with gratitude and breathe in their scents, tuck their wispy blond hair across their foreheads, and kiss their noses as they sleep.

I need my heart reshaped and vision reframed so that I can see all the good that comes with growing old. When I was twenty, I was afraid of thirty. But in reality, I love who I'm becoming. If I could, I would tell my younger self that growing up is nothing to be afraid of. It is actually so good. I'd tell my younger self that life gets better with age. In my youth, I was like a young tree with several stakes poked into the ground holding it secure. The stakes were things in my life that I held on to for strength. I needed them in order to be safe: church, parents, personality, sisters, marriage, friends, education, motherhood, and my extensive travel itinerary. Over the last twenty years, each of these stakes was snapped. Each person or thing I depended on broke. In desperation, I tried to cling to them, but one by one, they didn't give me the security they once had. While I felt lost, drowning, depressed, and insignificant, God was actually growing me. When I thought I couldn't carry on, God carried me. He was loving me through those snapped stakes and into someone stronger. I was flourishing from a sapling to an oak tree. I'm growing older and into a more beautiful version of myself. I'm becoming who I've always been meant to be. I am so much more faithful, brave, and forgiving. I'm so much more kind, gracious, and whole. I would never go back to twenty, twenty-five, or thirty. I want to keep growing older. I want to be as solid and calm and humble as an oak tree whose long arms extend out and over, sheltering all who need reprieve. Growing older is so good. I can't wait to see who I'll be when I'm sixty. I can't wait to meet her. I'm sure of one thing: She would tell me, "Savor and give thanks." The same words I'd say to myself at twenty.

I've always looked at growing older with doom, but in reality, it is my destiny. Growing old is the goal. The goal for me is to give this one life I've been given everything I've got. It is to leave a legacy of love. I'll point to the later years of my life and fall forward. I will savor it and be savored in it. I'll turn forty and be the one singing loudest, taking every moment in. I'm certain I'll still be afraid, but no matter what, I'll be saying "thank you" over and over. I'll say it until I lose my voice. I'll say it until my skin is translucent and my legs shake. I'll say it with every passing year and up to my dying breath. Breathe in: Savor. Breathe out: Thank you.

I have to live in the vulnerable trust that God will continue to carry me into eternity the way He has carried me since birth.

29 WEEKS

An Invitation to Trauma

e only packed one suitcase for our two-night stay in Cabo San Lucas. Our flight landed at 2:30 p.m. on a Tuesday just days after Thanksgiving. We were headed to a land where poverty and beauty collide with cheap beachfront hotel rooms, smorgasbords of buffet tables, and bottomless drinks. Sam and I kissed our kids goodbye and caught a flight to where I was going to shoot a wedding, and Sam would be officiating it. The two-and-a-half-hour flight from San Diego to Mexico was dreamy; we were alone, kidless, and carefree. We toasted on the plane, Sam with a Bloody Mary and me with cranberry juice over ice. I was 29 weeks pregnant. Walking through the airport's sliding glass doors into Cabo's sweet sunshine, I felt warm heat kissing my skin. I was on vacation, a much-needed break, a space in the chaos of holidays, meal planning, hosting, and meetings. I could exhale, releasing the weight of managing little lives—school schedules, naps, and the dinging of the dryer. It would be our last trip alone for a very long time, and we were anxious to let this space be a sanctuary before the birth of our fourth baby, a little girl.

After breathing in the salty air at sunset and devouring the dessert bar, I felt something inside of me start to shift—a contraction. Unmistakable. I tried to shake it off with cold water and good thoughts. Sam and I decided to turn in for the evening. On the edge of a random envelope stuffed at the bottom of my purse, I jotted down the first number of many: 7:35.

7:35, 7:42, 7:45, 7:51, 7:53. My contractions were strong and stiff, the momentum swelling and stopping, swelling and stopping. The oceanic rhythm of labor made its way through my body. Time pressed forward, pressure pushed down on me, panic welled up inside of me. The contractions increased in power. I kept one eye on my phone timer and another on Sam, wondering what we were going to do, wondering where we would go, knowing what we were about to face was something that was so far beyond us. As my phone ticked away, I jotted down the next series of numbers: 10:45, 10:47, 10:50, 10:54, 10:57. I held my breath and prayers held me. Unexpected contractions pulsed fear and anxiety through my body like a massive surge of energy plowing me over.

Sam started to sort things into a bag. "We are going to the hospital," he said calmly. The clock read 12:04 a.m. I gripped my arms around my baby and followed Sam to the lobby, waiting for our ride to the emergency room. We were uncertain of where an actual hospital was and how to communicate with the hotel bellboy what was going on. Warm tears were stewing, pushing up, and slipping over and down my face. My baby was inching her way into the world, squirming around, anxious for new oxygen. Sam was trying to navigate our driver through unknown streets with a map he couldn't read, on roads that seemed to go in circles. Every two minutes a surge of pressure inside my belly doubled me over. The too-frequent speed bumps made our little car bounce, and I pressed every finger down into the side of my leg, lips tucked in under my teeth, tears swiftly brushed away, bracing for the next road hazard, the next inevitable contraction. I looked out my window into the darkness of the Mexican night, at the array of polka-dot streetlights that made everything look so happy. It was eerily beautiful. My mind raced with numbers — when did the contractions start; how long were they lasting; what level of pain was I in? The loudest number running through my mind was 29. 29 weeks. I was 29 weeks along, only 29.

We parked and went inside. It wasn't a hospital. It was a clinic. An urgent care facility. I was wheeled into a room bright with fluorescent lights and pink walls, waiting for the doctor to arrive. I was instantly strapped to monitors and asked about my history of premature labor and when I had my last period and why I had three previous C-sections. In the waiting, I watched my skin tighten and stretch, move in and move out, muscles gripping in and around me, making it hard to breathe.

We watched our baby move on the ultrasound machine in greens and grays. The screen was like a monitor I had in middle school. The doctor watched my womb contract, her hand applying pressure around all the parts of my baby girl, from my ribs to my hips and around my lower back. An IV was injected, medicines started, and shots left me wheezing in pain. The waiting never seemed to stop: waiting for the next contraction, waiting for our doctor in the U.S. to call, waiting for test results to turn out negative, waiting to hear her heartbeat, waiting for insurance to clear, waiting for this nightmare to pass so we could go back to the hotel and the open dessert bar. But the waiting never stopped and neither did the contractions.

Two doctors were beside our bed, looking to each other, trying to communicate as clearly as they could, with slowness and serious-ness in their eyes: Our baby was coming. There was nothing they could do to stop what had already begun. Our 29-week-old baby would be born here, in Mexico.

Just like that, the room went stone cold. I looked over at Sam, my strength, my solid friend for so many years. His hands pressed against his face, tears falling and quickly wiped away, his head for-ward, heart hunching over his knees, his spine bending like a hook curving in over his fear. He turned his head away from me, trying to find composure. But I could see through him like an x-ray. I could see his panic. Except for the sound of our baby's heart beating on the monitor, we wept in silence.

The room started to spin with the blur of hospital lights, my whole world suddenly in dire need of reprieve. Nurses tapped on the door, poked my skin, helped me pee in a bedpan. Receptionists asked for insurance cards and signatures and authorizations. Sam, in military mode, making decisions, trying to interpret Spanish with hand motions. I was bleeding unexpectedly, and the unit went into code red to stabilize me; fortunately, they did. My baby was still safe. She was still alive. But she was coming.

We needed a miracle—an absolute, out-of-the-sky, current-day, David-and-Goliath, God-sized miracle. We needed to get home. We needed my contractions to stop. We needed a plane that would take us to a specific hospital in the States. We needed money— a lot of money—we needed our insurance to approve of the air ambulance, and we had eight hours to make this all happen. We had a small window of time, and if that window passed, the doctors would deliver my 29-week-old baby girl via C-section in this ill-equipped urgent care clinic. The doctor assured me the hospital was capable of taking care of a premature baby. She had delivered one successfully in all her years. One. *Only* one.

Over the next several hours, I watched Sam through the slat of my hospital bed begging our insurance to approve a plane. I heard him agonizing with the Blue Cross representative about the conditions we were in, asking if they would take responsibility if our girl didn't live. Sometimes he had one phone in each hand, talking with one person and texting another, the door of our room constantly swinging open and shut. I lay back in my bed, head resting, feeling my womb contracting, tightening, and releasing, over and over again.

And just when I'd lose hope or when despair would wash over me, I'd hear the ding of my phone. I'd look down to see messages of encouragement or prayers from across the border. So many voices echoing in unison, "We are praying, holding you and your baby before Jesus." The prayers and texts came flooding in like water, pouring out protection and light over our hospital room, filling our hearts with hope. With each message I'd be able to breathe again because those voices of comfort became for me a pathway to see through the thick impossible. By the grace of so many prayers, we were sustained. We were held. And in that little pink room in Cabo San Lucas we were bombarded with love. A love that came after us, pursued us, and smashed through borders and boundaries and foreign languages just to reach us.

It was the prayers of many and the miracles of the One that brought us home. Without explanation a plane landed, without hesitation money was wired, and when contractions shouldn't have stopped, they did. Paramedics strapped me onto a stretcher and took us thirty miles to the nearest airport, IV in, with a headache so severe it pounded my eyes shut. The men lifted the board I was tied to through the small door of the tiny plane. They rocked the stretcher back and forth, forward and backward, like a new driver attempting to parallel park. Like a dropped pick inside the body of a guitar, I was jostled over and over again, trying to find a way to freedom. I was forced to open my eyes and look up. What I saw silenced every ounce of fear I was fighting against. I saw the moon. The moon, clear and full and bright and majestic, completely unmoved by my circumstances. The same moon I see from my bedroom window calling closure to my day. The same moon God so graciously designed to mandate rest for our weary bodies. The moon like an explosion in the starless sky, saying, "Be still." The moon, a bullet bursting through my restlessness, shocking me into awe and the absolute reality that God was in control, always, even in Mexico.

I spent several days in the hospital in San Diego and was sent home on bed rest. Little Hannaly Grace July made it to 38 weeks in my womb and screamed a healthy, ear-piercing "I'm alive" when the doctor pulled her from the hole across my abdomen. Everything turned out okay. But I wasn't. Some part of me was still trapped in Mexico. I couldn't sleep imagining "what could have happened." I could have died. My baby could have died. The worst-case scenario could have happened. It shocked my entire system. I was left trembling. It felt so wrong to call it *trauma* because, in reality, the best-case scenario happened.

I reserve the word *trauma* for murder and sexual abuse and veterans home from war. My experience in Mexico can't be labeled a trauma because my baby girl lived. But there is big "T" trauma and little "t" trauma. Big "T" trauma is a life-altering situation: a sudden death, a massive accident, a natural disaster. Little "t" trauma is anything that disrupts life, causing helplessness or loss of control: sickness, job loss, financial troubles, a breakup, even planning a wedding or moving. Then there are events in life that just don't fit into any category. I put these things in the bad-thing-that-happened box. Somehow, if I can find a place for things to fit, it just makes me feel better. Mexico was a little "t" trauma. The aftermath of that experience left me with daily aftershocks, making it hard to navigate normal life again. My un-dealt-with trauma was becoming fertile soil for toxic thoughts to take root. I kept feeling out of control, anxious, afraid. I felt like a part of me was still in that pink room under interrogating lights. I've spent so much of my life stuck in the "bad things that happened." I left parts of myself behind because they made me feel ugly or heavy or dumb. So much shame and guilt circle certain parts of my story like crows lurking over a corpse. But I don't want to leave myself behind anymore. I don't want to be stuck in Mexico. What use am I to people I love if true parts of me are trapped back in my younger years? I want to be here, present, in real-life time with all of me.

We each have a trauma or a "bad thing that happened": an accident, a death, a disapproving father, an angry mother, an illness, a pastor who failed you, a divorce, a coach who shamed you, a friend who left you, a boy who hurt you, a miscarriage that wrecked you. No matter how horrible or small or painful or disgusting it was, stop running from it. Stop pretending it's okay or isn't there, because that trauma is going to bury you in lies. It will taunt you with "you're never good enough, you should have known better, you messed up—again—you don't deserve happiness, no wonder no one loves you, it's your fault, be quiet." Stop running. I beg of you. Sit down. Stay.

Whether the trauma happened five minutes or fifty-five years ago, make it your life's mission to get help. Even if everyone already knows, even when the meals stop arriving at your doorstep and people move on, keep asking for a hand to hold. Speak your trauma for the rest of your life because it is a healing salve: your voice and God's voice, enmeshed in your story of salvation. God is relentless to love you through that "bad thing that happened." There is a battle for your soul. A spiritual war to keep parts of you stuck in pain. God is ferociously fighting for you to become untangled from the grip that it has on you. God's love will never leave any part of you behind in your trauma. He doesn't just go after lost, hurting, broken, abandoned, and forgotten people. God goes after the lost, hurting, broken, abandoned, and forgotten parts of you. He goes after your trauma, not to torture you, but to love you into wholeness. Stay with your trauma until the sting dissipates. Stay with it until God invites you to turn around and offer your hand to someone else walking through a story similar to what you've just come through.

So even when it wasn't easy, I kept processing what happened in Mexico. God always brought me back to that little clinic in the middle of nowhere. I wept and recounted the situation. I cried and told the story again and again until it didn't make me shake anymore. I experienced love like a deep, powerful force. My soul was like loose, wet concrete, God pressed His handprint across my chest, and I was made stronger through the drying process, through the healing. He infused love into my trauma like that IV into my arm in Mexico. Right into the crease of my skin, love medicine streamed through damaged veins, sending love into what had been shattered. This love made the world stop and wait for me and my baby to get home. This love helped me unpack my trauma after she was born. Slowly, the sting started to shift. The trauma became less of a trigger for my fear and more about God's story of rescue. When I became pregnant again, three years later, with my fifth baby, my trauma was poked again. Anxiety walked with me through parts of my pregnancy, but so did Jesus. I stayed with my fear, and God stayed with me. Mea Joy is my encore baby. I like to think that God loved what He saw in our family, cheered, and wanted more of it (but yes, she was a surprise). I followed doctors' orders religiously and stayed within the U.S. border all the way until she was born.

THE MOMS WE LOVE CLUB

An Invitation to Bleed

I was restless. I couldn't sleep. It wasn't because of my baby or our half-finished bathroom. It was because I stumbled across a GoFundMe on Facebook that completely wrecked me. A woman named Lindsay was battling for her life against status migrainosus, a disease that attacks her mind, making breathing unbearable. Lindsay spends twenty-three and a half hours of her day in horrific, brain-throbbing, body-aching, unimaginable pain. It's a migraine that never, ever stops. Their GoFundMe described how her husband, Bobby, carries her to the shower, brushes her teeth, cares for their son, and soothes her to sleep (a task that sometimes takes hours). While I venture about my day, Lindsay is confined to a dark prison, sweating, rocking in pain, and using every ounce

193

of her energy to manage the monster inside her mind. There is no cure. None. Without a miracle, Lindsay will spend the rest of her life in body arrest to this disease.

She is a mom, just like me. Before the onset of this disease, she traveled the world, chased beauty, took care of Bobby (suffering from Crohn's disease), and raised her little boy. She is gorgeous, young, kind, and good. One day, she woke up with a headache that put her in bed for the rest of her life. I just couldn't fathom the horror of a disease like this. I couldn't sleep. I thought of Lindsay that night and every night after that, for over a year, before I did anything for her.

I thought about ways I could help her: Could I make her a meal, clean her bathroom, carpool her son to school? I felt desperate to help and desperately helpless. I didn't have a single thing to give her that would relieve the pressure. But, night after night, as I tried to sleep, Lindsay would drift into my thoughts and slowly drift out. I couldn't complain about anything in my life. I didn't have that right. Lindsay, the same age as me, couldn't lift her head up without help. Yet she was still whispering the name of Jesus.

So, I'd pray for her. I'd live better because of her. I'd hold her before God and beg Him to manage the massive amount of pain pressing up against her. I looked at my life, raising five kids, home-schooling, and helping Sam give CPR to the church he was pastoring. I looked at my hands and how packed they were with schedules and grocery shopping and just plain surviving. I looked at how I spent my time washing dishes, wiping faces, and swiping through social media.

My love for photography was now a creative outlet on a little app called Instagram. I spent a lot of my in-between moments there, scrolling, commenting, liking, and making friends with people who were doing the same thing I was: mothering. "Instagram is a modern-day well for women," my dear friend Blair always says. It is where women chat, connect, share, gather, laugh, encourage, and inspire. I didn't have a huge platform, but what I had, I gave. Birthed at the intersection of my bleeding heart for Lindsay, passion for photography, and online community came @themomswelove club. It became the perfect place for love to grow. At this Instagram well, I invited people to stay, share, pray, and give to Lindsay.

The Moms We Love Club became a place for the brokenhearted and the healers to dwell. Once a month, I share a story and a picture of a mother in desperate need of love. The first month was Lindsay Earle. Every "member" (follower) in the club posted the same picture of Lindsay lying beside her son, Clive. Her eyes were draped closed with a cloth as Clive innocently peered out the window and rested on his momma's chest. It's a powerful image that makes you stop scrolling, lean in, and question what is happening. The more people posted, the more love Lindsay felt. The more people shared, the more prayer she received. The more people saw the image, the more money was raised.

The first month, we raised $14,000 for Lindsay. I was crying on the floor shocked after I saw the total. This momma, who lived every day in the dark for over six years, was seen. People who endure the long, unbreakable, dark alley of suffering somehow get lost in the shadows. They become the forgotten ones. When people can't fix the problem, they slowly move on. Isolation sets in. My greatest hope isn't to raise a lot of money, but to remind these mothers in the most inescapable-hell-on-earth nightmares that they aren't alone. We are with them. God is for them.

After Lindsay was Lori. Lori was a mom to five boys (ages 9, 7, 5, 13 months, and 3 months old) when her husband, Steve, was hit by a drunk driver while riding his bike on Super Bowl Sunday. He was left to die when a stranger found him. Steve is now a quadriplegic, confined to a wheelchair and unable to speak, move, or reach for Lori's hand. He can't lift his babies or throw them over his shoulders playfully. Lori does everything. The image we all posted of Lori on Instagram is striking. She and four of the boys are pushing Steve's enormous wheelchair while the youngest is propped on his lap. You can't help but break and bend over in ache for this family, for Lori. People around the world posted, prayed, and donated. We raised close to $80,000. I can't tell Lori's story without crying.

After Lori were Nicole, Jamie, and Stacey. Moms who had a stillborn, a boy with Down syndrome diagnosed with leukemia, and a son with a death sentence called Batten disease. We've supported moms with breast cancer, children with rare diseases, and widows. We've supported moms who've now passed into eternity and children who slipped into heaven far too early. I've wept in the shower. I've had long conversations with Jesus about how unfair life is. I've practically begged people to post a single picture on their feed because it will, without a doubt, change a life. Sharing an image takes twelve seconds but impacts a hurting momma forever.

The Moms We Love Club feed is everything painful and beautiful in the world, the good and horrible holding hands.

I viewed this online club as a marriage of so many things I cared about. It was a harmonious merger of photography, networking, and social media with my heartbreak for moms who are in the heaviest throes of life. All these combined make my heart come alive. Our world can be so cutthroat. Everyone is screaming: get bigger, grow taller, speak louder, climb higher. I get sucked right into the vortex of these lies chanting, "If you just try a little bit harder, you can reach your dreams." I get anxious, wondering if I'm doing enough. I pace and panic under the pressure to do it all.

This club has changed me. It has changed my understanding of my calling, vocation, and purpose. I'm not called to build an empire; I'm invited to dig a well. I'm invited to stay right where my heart bleeds and offer the thirsty water. Whether the well is words or motherhood or feeding the poor—dig deeper. Whether the well is to end sex trafficking or education or counseling—stay there. Whether it is baking or being on the PTA or nursing or running a business—the place where your heart beats is exactly where Jesus is inviting you to be. Be where your heart bleeds.

At the well, everything comes together. God's design is the union of my desires and the world's needs. My passions and heartbreaks are necessary at the well. All I have to do is be faithful to stay, dig, and offer water to the thirsty ones God brings. It might be one person or a million. It might be a world-altering cause or a small city project. It might be the neighborhood kid who keeps knocking, the homeless man on the corner, joining a movement to end slavery, the widow who lives down the street, the hungry bodies that keep showing up, or the teacher with an edge. When you offer someone hope, that one person is all that matters.

I'm not sure what the future of The Moms We Love Club is. All I know is that God keeps bringing women who need reprieve. I don't really know how, month after month, money is raised and the forgotten feel found, but it keeps happening. It really is a miracle. Every month it is hard to see suffering so up close. Love isn't always easy, but it is always right.

I've never met Lindsay, but I love her. She lives right inside my heart. I know she's been in and out of the hospital, and her health continues to decline. I know there aren't any more walls to knock down or surgeries to try. I know there are absolutely no words that could soothe the story she lives in. I don't intend to try. But I'll walk with her. I'll shine a light in her direction as long as I live. The truth is, I haven't changed her life as much as she has changed mine. She has gracefully and courageously chosen to stay at her well. It's meshed with tragedy and fear and pain and Jesus. When I pop onto her Instagram feed and read her posts, it's like I'm drinking fresh water. It's like my bleeding heart is held, and I'm drinking water straight from the cupped hands of Christ. Even though she is imprisoned in darkness, she has become for me a light leading me to the place where Jesus lives. He is always at the well.

21

ORANGE

An Invitation to Be Loved

efore I could swim, I jumped off the diving board of a neighbor's pool. I remember the moments underwater in slow motion. The glitter of the sun through the rippling water, my arms reaching, fingertips barely touching the surface, where air was my rescue. Seconds felt like forever. I heard the desperate screams of my mom trapped behind screen doors, her voice distant and echoing. I wasn't afraid. My body was still as I watched the water separate me from the sky. And then, when my eyes closed, my sister lifted me from the water. When no one else could reach me, Leonie swam into the deep waters. All at once I could breathe, the taste of oxygen in my lungs. I don't think about that day often; I don't remember much else before or after that moment, but I remember the way the water moved over me, washing and reflecting the summer sun. Drowning can be a silent death. No screams, no flailing arms, no panicked knees doing bicycle spins. Only silence, limbs sleeping, a weight sinking in the deep end.

So many of us are drowning and don't know how to be saved anymore or have given up trying. We've done all we can do to stop the sinking, but the angst we feel is slowly pushing us farther down. When Christian answers don't suffice and church isn't meeting felt needs, our souls begin to drift. Some of us have exhausted every spiritual discipline and listened to every podcast, yet our hearts are left weary and unsatisfied. We feel desperately stuck. The invitation isn't to get unstuck, but to settle in. The spiritual wall we smash up against isn't a wall we have to climb over or knock down or fall asleep at. It is there for a reason. In fact, it isn't a wall at all, but a well where Jesus meets us. We think we are there alone with our secrets, hurt, apathy, boredom, confusion, and disappointment. But Jesus is there and invites us to stay with the truth of our hearts and the water He is offering. God invites us into deeper communion and intimacy with Him.

The invitation is to crawl up into our Father's lap, letting His arms wrap us up. We are like tired children at the end of the day, with our worn-out bodies and watery eyes, heads resting on His shoulder, listening as He whispers hope into our cracked hearts. "I've got you. . . . I love you. . . . I'm not letting you go. I am for you. I am not a checklist or burden or something to get done. I've only ever been about being with you."

This is staying. This is John 15:4: "Stay joined to me and I will stay joined to you." It is so simple. It requires no effort, it just is. We stay with God and He stays with us like a Father with a child. They are always united and connected. No emancipation, no distance, no degree of disapproval, no time lost can ever separate souls that are joined together. When we are born again as beloved children of God, we are forever heart-held by Him. There is no work to gain acceptance or get approval, no control or convincing needed. Once a child is born to a father, there is nothing that can break the bond. We are burrowed right into His bosom.

God wraps all of our wounds until our souls can see straight again. He won't let us fade into the shadows or let fears swallow us whole without a constant nudge and pull and push or small tap on our hearts to abide. He will never let the hurt in our hearts subside until every bound-up muscle is held effortlessly in the wounds that bled our redemption into being. We don't invite Jesus into our hearts; we are invited into His. Every single ache is a divine invitation to be loved, to be known, and to be made whole.

The more I unwrap the wounds, worn-out bandages trailing behind me, the more I see how my pain leads me home like bread crumbs in a fairy tale. The more I stay and let the pain have a voice—the more I speak the truth of who I really am with God and others, the closer to home I get. I'm seeing how in my loneliest and darkest moments, I was invited in. All my wandering and fog and confusion was the way God was actually growing me. The more I live open and vulnerable to my messiness, my fatigue and shame, my embarrassment and past, my happiness and awkwardness, my uniqueness and voice, the more I realize that I am not writing my story but I am actually living out the glorious story that has already been written in me. His story penning mine.

The urge to speak now screams through my blood. I wrestle to find my voice, to understand my past, and to fill in the blank voids that fall like dark blankets over certain seasons of my life. When the love of God lifts the veil from the hazy places within, His voice beating in sync with mine, wholeness is birthed and reborn again and again. So I speak and I seek out the hidden corners that taunt me. I stay, even when I want to run. I follow my resistance all the way to freedom. I let my ongoing story develop and I keep speaking. I stay and tell my story, admitting that I've made a million damaging mistakes along the way. I speak until my voice shakes because then I am really speaking. My voice is unique. My voice speaks in shades of orange like the granite gorges of the Grand Canyon. It has texture and depth and vibrancy and resiliency. My voice and the voice of God have found an intersection, a center, a dwelling place. Here, I am alive. There is little I long for more in life. I want to be alive with the God who is fully alive in me.

I have one purpose in life. One. It isn't to glorify God or make disciples. It isn't to be a good mom or wife or friend. My purpose isn't to be enough, to be needed, to be safe, unique, or significant. I'm not required to have all knowledge and understanding or to enthusiastically engage the world. No, the goal of my life isn't even to find peace or to be perfect. My one and only purpose in life is to be loved by God. That's it. It is the foundation, the starting line, first and foremost. My purpose begins with God pursuing me, staying with me, loving me. It's why and how we were created. If I miss this, I miss it all. Everything else follows. Everything is birthed from this reality. It is a springboard for our calling, vocation, and relationships. That is why God pursues us to the very depths of our beings. Our hearts need to know this, not just as an idea in our heads, but as a fact that sustains us as effortlessly as we breathe.

I am so tempted to make it more than love. I want to work or earn or prove or gain love. I want to stuff, fill, and consume anything that mimics God's love. I so easily forget that God loves me. I know He loves me, but in order to help me believe it, God takes me on a radical journey into my heart. As I follow Him into the fragile, deep end of my story, He is there, waking me up to true self-awareness of my motivations and desires. He awakens my heart to His love. Even with all the pain and heartache that my story holds, I wouldn't change it. If my story is taken, my deep understanding of God's love for me is taken too.

God invites me to stay with myself, others, and himself in truth. That's why on Sunday mornings I sing and weep, "Prone to wander, Lord, I feel it, prone to leave the God I love. Here's my heart, Lord, take and seal it, seal it for thy courts above."[7] I plead with God to keep me close because I know that I know that I know I will forget, lose sight, and slip back into getting love from anything else but Him. I know how quickly I dismiss my feelings, avoid my issues, pretend to be okay, and try to fix myself. So, again, I invite every part of me back to the table of my soul. Here, there is exhale. Here, there is wholeness. I stay with my pain, feelings, shame, and struggles because God uses them to bring me back to His love. I do the disciplines, get weak in awe of creation, raise my children, and speak my sins because God uses them to bring me back to my fundamental purpose in life: to be loved.

From when my sister rescued me from the deep end of the swimming pool, to coordinating Orange Wednesday in college, to rocking my babies back to sleep, God's invitation has always been the same: stay awake to love. From the beginning to the end, from the littlest to the largest, from the empty to the most mysterious moments of my life, it all has purpose. God is weaving His redemptive story into mine.

When summer's heat manages to sweep sand into every corner of my shoes and car and white sheets, I stay. When fall brings a chill that burns leaves into brightness and prunes our rosebushes bare, I stay. When long winters are marked by sipping tea and missing my grandma, who always made room at the table for one more, I stay. When spring bursts in with bougainvillea, its purples like vibrant firecrackers, climbing so high, waving frantically toward the heavens, "We are here. We are here. We are here," I stay.

When my tears fall effortlessly and silently in the dark of the back-row pew, and when I think no one sees, I am reminded to enter, open, and come back to my story. The beginning, middle, and end are always the same. It is a never-ending, grace-breathing story for all mankind. Love, a gentle cadence that keeps the world in motion. God's story is the endlessly poetic, patient, and perfect invitation to stay with Him because He is always, till the end of eternity, staying with me.

Stay awake

to love.

DISCUSSION QUESTIONS

Thoughts to Consider

The Way Hearts Die

- Are there parts of your story that feel unknown or wordless or hard to explain?
- Is your tendency to work harder, withdraw, or walk away from your faith?
- What parts of your story are you most resistant to exploring?

Chapter One: Chapel and Charlie

- Who are the people in your life who make you feel like you truly belong?
- How is God meeting you in places where you feel like you are on the outside?
- Is there a person in your life who has made you feel like you belong?

Chapter Two: The Guard Shack

- How have you viewed mistakes in your life? Through the lens of love or condemnation?
- What idols have you built your life on?
- Describe what the "perfect" you looks like.

Chapter Three: My Addiction

- What is your addiction?
- Are there people in your life whom you feel the need to fix or save?
- Do you have things in your life that you use to hide from others (spiritual disciplines, children, being strong)?
- Where are areas in your life that you can ask for help?

Chapter Four: The Lake

- Describe a physical place in your life that holds deep meaning.
- Can you name a few people who have impacted and encouraged you to be more real?
- In your life, are you becoming more vulnerable or less? Why?

Chapter Five: Naked Mango Eating

- What do you use to fill your loneliness?
- When and where do you experience your greatest loneliness, and how do you avoid that feeling?
- How have you used prayer and the spiritual disciplines to hide from God?

Chapter Six: Fox Island

- Would you describe your relationship with Jesus as hard or easy?
- In what parts of your life are you experiencing living water flowing effortlessly, and where do you feel stuck?
- How do you experience the truth of who you are: with eyes of love or with self-hatred?

Chapter Seven: The Coffee Shop

- Take a moment to examine your ability and desire to really hear others.
- What strategies do you use to keep from really listening?
- Is it hard for you to let other people have their own story, or do you fear the story they walk will negatively affect you?

Chapter Eight: My Friend Sam

- Can you describe a time when you have experienced rejection?
- In what ways is fear holding you back from pursuing a dream, a person, or an experience?
- What dreams in your life are you holding on to so tightly that surrendering them feels painful?

Chapter Nine: When He Proposed

- What expectations did you take into marriage?
- How has marriage disappointed or surprised you?
- What do the weeds of your marriage look like?
- Do you feel safe letting God roam in your weeds?

Chapter Ten: 547 East 6th Ave

- Is there someone in your life who has been like a Papa John for you?
- List a few ways God tangibly provided for you in the past.
- How can you be a placeholder of heaven for others today?

Chapter Eleven: Showing Up

- Do you have a dream you are scared to admit?
- How do you find validation?

- Do you feel seen?
- What are you *not* showing up for in life right now?

Chapter Twelve: Glow

- Who in your life glows, and why?
- How do you experience your fear, with eyes of fear or with eyes of love?
- What voices are loudest and quietest at the table of your soul?

Chapter Thirteen: Sushi and *Friday Night Lights*

- What areas of your life (past or present) do you think you're failing at?
- What areas in your life are you rushing to get through, and why?
- What do you use to cover your shame?
- Do you experience God as being delighted in you? If not, how do you think He feels about you right now?

Chapter Fourteen: What Rissa Said

- When you think about your finances, do you have anxiety? If so, can you describe why?

- Do you feel like God is nudging you to give more? If so, where?
- Who is a person in your life who is generous with you? What does that feel like?

Chapter Fifteen: Noelle Hope

- Share a story from your life when you had to wait and saw God's hand in your story.
- Describe some of your strategies to avoid, fill, or fast-forward waiting.
- Is there a "waiting room" in your life right now that is painful?

Chapter Sixteen: Exposed

- What areas of your life are you afraid to let others see?
- Are there places in your daily life that feel insignificant and unseen?
- Describe the different ways you hide from God and others.
- Can you identify true guilt versus false guilt in your life?

Chapter Seventeen: Old Spaghetti Factory

- Name a master bedroom friend and tell what makes them that kind of friend.

- Do you have a friendship that has caused deep pain?
- Is there a friend in your life that you need to take to Jesus?

Chapter Eighteen: Savor

- How do you feel about aging?
- What small details of your day are you grateful for?
- What would you tell your younger self?

Chapter Nineteen: 29 Weeks

- Do you have unprocessed trauma ("T" or "t") in your life?
- Have you ever felt stuck in a trauma? If not, what has helped you move through it well?
- Can you explore ways you can find healing from the "bad things that have happened" to you?
- Is there someone in your life you can help who is going through a trauma similar to one you've been through?

Chapter Twenty: The Moms We Love Club

- What makes your heart bleed?
- How do you see that passion as a way God can use you in the world?
- Describe your well and how God is inviting you to offer others life-giving water from it.

Chapter Twenty-One: Orange

- Describe where you are drowning or stuck in your faith.
- What are your aches today?
- Do you experience, know, or believe that God loving you is the purpose of your life?
- Describe what staying with God looks like for you.

ACKNOWLEDGMENTS

Endless thanks to my parents. To my mom, who has always let me twirl, dance, and wear clothes that didn't match. Thank you for letting me sit on the counter beside you while you cooked. Thank you for reading each word written a dozen times and for the pencil scratches that made my writing better. Thank you for always encouraging me to chase my dreams. Tea is always best when it is shared with you. To my dad, who reminds me I've always been wanted.

Endless thanks to my sisters. Leonie, for always accepting and advising me. Malina, for the way you make me laugh and love life. Wanida, thank you for your friendship, honesty, courage, and constant encouragement. Thank you for being a safe place for the real me to stay. I miss living life with you.

Endless thanks to my childhood friends: Becca, Kara, Mindy, and Krissa. Thank you for carrying my cot to Jesus—again and again and again. I love our birthday club.

Endless thanks to each of you who let me tell your stories in this book. Your stories have shaped me into who I am.

Endless thanks to my extended family (Paschall, Maneevone, Kubo, and Redding). Thank you for being threads that knit me together. Thank you, Joe, Nate, Josh, and Dan, for being the brothers I never had. Thank you, Rebecca (Charlie), for years of kindness. Brenda, thank you for being such a kind grandma, for your cranberry juice, and for raising such an incredible son.

Endless thanks to my grandma Millie Redding, who is with Jesus. She was a friend to everyone, but especially to me. She is so deeply missed.

Endless thanks to Katie, January, and Jessica. You are my sisters. I love you.

Endless thanks to Krissa. When the ink was still hot from the printer, you helped me catch all the mistakes. Your loyalty to me means more than you will ever know.

Endless thanks to Jessie Chatigny, Rissa Poling, Molly Keating, Rachel Redding, Katie Paschall, and Jerusha Clark for reading my heart on paper so early on.

Endless thanks to my dear friends Anna, Mackenzie, Colleen, Jenni, and Becky. You have shaped my understanding of God through our life experiences and long conversations.

Endless thanks to the many beautiful women who endorsed this book. I have such a deep respect for each one of you. Thank you, Katherine, for teaching me and the world how to suffer strong.

Endless thanks to Emily P. Freeman for offering me wisdom about my writing right when I needed it most.

Endless thanks to Jamin and Kristin Goggin for cheering me on and being such kind and supportive friends. Thank you, Kristin, for all the sweets and shared life experiences. I'm with you.

Endless thanks to Ashley. Thank you for generously pouring out love into my life. Thank you for adoring my girls and loving my boys. You matter and your story isn't done yet.

Endless thanks to John Coe, Betsy Barber, Judy TenEslhof, and Steve Porter for helping me grow up in Christ.

Endless thanks to Bryan Vandragt. Without your incredible guidance and deep compassion and sharp discernment, my life would be drastically different.

Endless thanks to my first counselor, Helyn Fay, who is with Jesus. She gave a young girl a place to sit and cry and speak. I am forever grateful for her presence in my life.

Endless thanks to Blair Fabry and Debbie Daniel. Thank you for always offering me wisdom and a light to my path.

Endless thanks to my beautiful Instagram community. Thank you for reminding me I am not alone. I'm so grateful for Tiffany, Meredith, Manda, Aly, Leslie, Yvette, Melissa (and many others!) who have become my real-life friends because of this big/little app.

Endless thanks to every single mom featured on @themomswe loveclub. You are my heroes and your stories are sacred. Thank you to all the photographers, followers, and friends who have helped me make this club possible (Christina, Mindy, Jennifer, Jesse, Colleen).

Endless thanks to Rissa for speaking bold, beautiful God-truth into my life, and to Jenn for years of friendship, memories, and teaching me about faith.

Endless thanks to my (in)courage writers. I respect each of you so much. I'm honored to write alongside you.

Endless thanks to the team at Bethany House, who helped make this book a reality (especially Ellen for your meticulous edits).

Endless thanks to Lisa Jackson, my agent. Thank you for saying yes to a girl you had never heard of. I'm so grateful you did.

Endless thanks to Katie Wolfe for your mentorship, prayers, and always reminding me to rest.

Endless thanks to Jennifer Dukes Lee, my editor. There are not enough words to express how grateful I am for you. Thank you for seeing me when I couldn't see myself. From cornfields to coastlines, God brings souls together. Thank you for giving my voice a microphone.

Endless thanks to past and present participants in the "Way of the Heart" and "Stay Awake to Love" course. You are each beautiful souls.

Endless thanks to my church family, Mission Hills Church. I'm so grateful to be a part of such a loving community. To the staff, elders, and their wives: thank you for embracing, supporting, and loving my family.

Endless thanks to my children. I see you, know you, and love you.

Manoah Nathaniel, may God use your strength to serve others.

Samuel Joseph Cash, may God use your sensitive spirit to buoy the broken.

Noelle Hope, may God use your creativeness to make space for love to grow.

Hannaly Grace July, may God use your spark to captivate hearts and awaken souls.

Mea Joy, may God use your light as a gift for all who need to see.

Lastly, endless thanks to my husband, Sam. You are my twin soul. You are my safety and my warmth. That night at the bookstore you told me you could only love me if you knew my entire story. No holding back, no secrets. You could only love me if you knew all of me. So I let you in. And from that moment on, you've been in love with me. You are the very reason I know that God loves me.

NOTES

1. Tim Keller, "The Wounded Spirit," sermon preached in New York City, December 5, 2004, https://verticallivingministries.com/2014/01/08/tim-keller-on-the-wounded-spirit-proverbs-series.

2. C.S. Lewis, *Mere Christianity* (New York: HarperCollins, 1952, 1980), 136–7.

3. Sara Groves, "From This One Place," *Fireflies and Songs*, Fair Trade, Columbia, and Integrity, 2009, compact disc.

4. Placide Cappeau, trans. John Sullivan Dwight, "O Holy Night," 1855, public domain.

5. Lisa-Jo Baker, "Why 'Mom' Is the Most Significant Job Title You Will Ever Have," *Lisa-Jo Baker*, December 5, 2012, http://lisajobaker.com/2012/12/why-mom-significant-job-title-will-ever.

6. G.K. Chesterton, *Orthodoxy* (CrossReach Publications, 2017), 37.

7. Robert Robinson, "Come Thou Fount of Every Blessing," 1757, public domain.

Anjuli Paschall grew up encircled by an orange grove in San Diego. After graduating from Point Loma Nazarene University, she earned her master's degree in spiritual formation and soul care from Talbot Seminary. She currently lives in Southern California with her husband, Sam (a pastor), and their five children. Anjuli is the founder of The Moms We Love Club and writes regularly for (in)courage. She loves chai tea, photography, the ocean, and the color orange.

Instagram: @lovealways.anjuli
@themomsweloveclub
www.anjulipaschall.com